MORE

Random Thoughts
of a

STUPID MAN

A Little Older but No More the Wiser

By
Mike Turnbull

More Random Thoughts of a Stupid Man Copyright © 2014 by Mike Turnbull
Rivershore Books
Cover design by Rivershore Books
Cover photo by Don Monroe
Author photo courtesy of author

ISBN-13: 978-0692226254
ISBN-10: 0692226257
First published in 2014

PRINTED IN THE UNITED STATES OF AMERICA

DEDICATION

More Random Thoughts of a Stupid Man is dedicated to my 2013-2014 Hibbing Community College Women's Basketball team.

Arianna, we all feel bad your injury kept you from finishing the season. You were missed by all of us, on and off the court.

Courtney, Christina, Danni, Taylor, and Ashlyn: I will never forget how the five of you stood up to the adversity and managed to play fourteen straight games with only five players and competed at a high level every night.

Every season, a team goes through its own unique journey. This season was truly unique, and I feel honored to have shared this journey with you.

Coach Mike Turnbull

"Toughest bunch of kids I've ever coached."
[Photo by Don Monroe]

CONTENTS

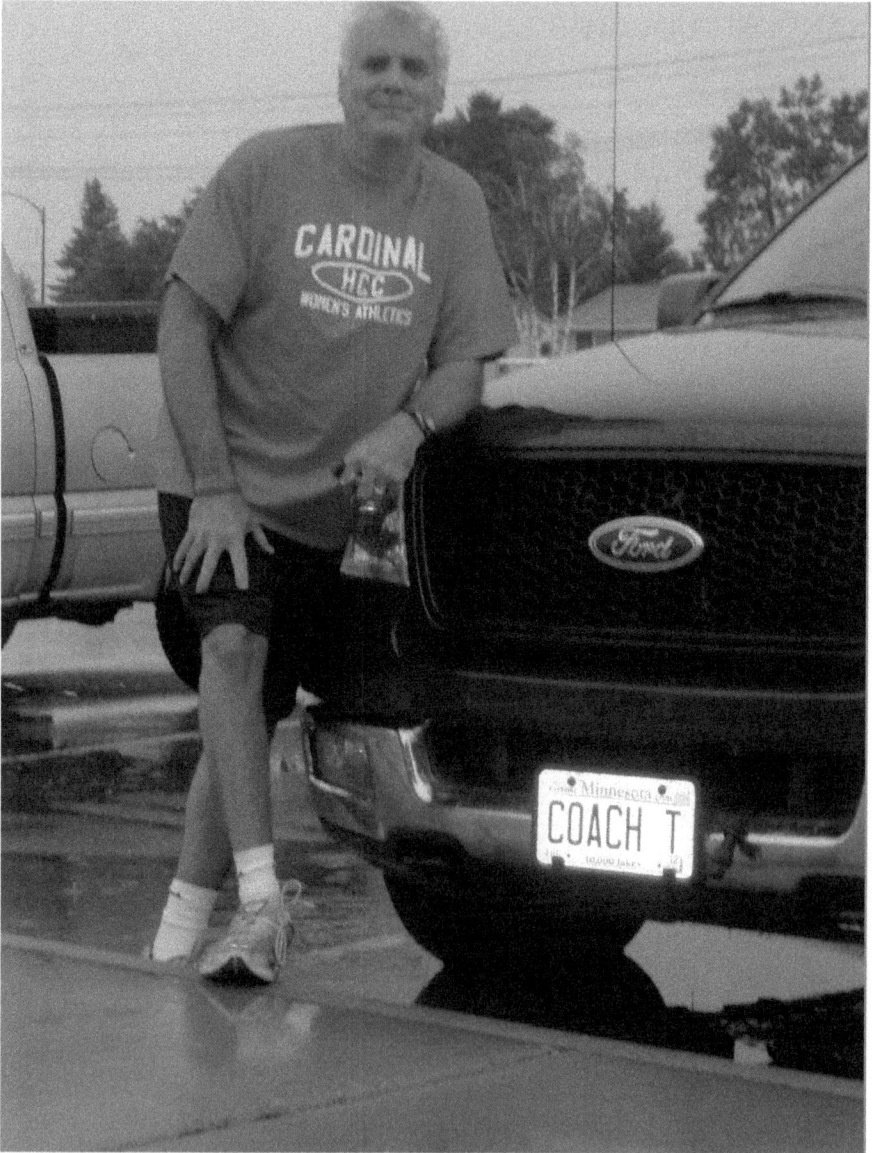

Mike Turnbull [Photo by Mike Flaten]

FOREWORD

My first book, *Random Thoughts of a Stupid Man,* was first re-leased in October of 2012. It was re-published by Rivershore Books in February of 2014. You might consider reading that before delving into this book. If not, if this one leaves you bewildered, go back and read the first one.

I have been encouraged by many people to continue writing, so I thought I'd continue the random thoughts as they come about in my daily life experiences.

Ed Nordskog, a dear friend, college roommate and teammate, and fellow author [Ed can actually write; I'm still trying to master the craft], told me that people will think you are smarter than you really are when they find out you have written a book. Despite what people think of me or may have said to me, I still do not feel any smarter, and I have seen and heard the word "Author" used in front of my name for over two years now.

My wife Pam and I were in Key West, Florida this past March and while there, toured Ernest Hemmingway's house with hundreds of other people. I honestly don't foresee a future where people will tour my house and be awestruck because Mike Turnbull the "Author" lived there.

That said, though, you are welcome to come and stay at our house. Pam and I own and live in the Mitchell-Tappan House Bed and Breakfast in Hibbing, Minnesota. The room rates are extremely reasonable, Pam cooks a great breakfast, and I'm sure you'll enjoy your stay. If you do come, please stop outside and say hi to the groundskeeper; that would be me.

This is probably the part of the Foreword where I am supposed to tell you what *More Random Thoughts of a Stupid Man* is about. I've got nothing! Right now I'm thinking I should have had Dr. Trent Janezich write the Foreword; he did a great job writing the Foreword for my first book.

I guess that is what *More Random Thoughts of a Stupid Man* is: a sharing of my life and the thoughts that enter my somewhat-demented mind on occasion. I'll admit, writing those thoughts has become more therapeutic than artful and brings me a deep feeling of comfort.

I can only hope that you enjoy the read! I also hope it leaves you wondering at times, "Did he just say that?" or "Did that really happen?" I'm here to tell you, I did just say that and that did just happen! I know this to be true, because I often catch myself wondering if I said that out loud or if I really did that. I also know my wife wonders the same things about me.

Please don't be too judgmental, I have already written two books in which I openly admit to being a "Stupid Man." As a matter of fact, just the other day I was watching Sports Center on ESPN; I have finally gotten pretty good at reading the ticker that streams across the bottom of the screen if I'm watching a large enough screen. I was thinking if ESPN collaborated with the Weather Channel and streamed our local weather report, I might never have to change the channel. If my wife wanted to get involved , maybe ESPN would allow her to put reminders on the ticker of things I need to do around the house or how I might use my time more constructively…or would that be just TMI?

If any of my current or ex-players or students are reading this book; yes, I just said TMI, and I know it stands for "Too much information!"

RANDOM THOUGHTS

7/16/2012

1] Members of congress have professed their displeasure with the U.S. Olympic Team members wearing uniforms made in China. I'm all for buying American-made products when I can, and I agree the Olympic Team should be wearing American products, but maybe the protesting congressional members should check their closets, office supplies and furniture, cell phones, clothing, cars, etc. before casting too many stones.

2] What is up with the weather this year? I live in north eastern Minnesota, and we had a mild winter with very little snow, 80-degree temperatures in the spring, and temperatures pushing 100 degrees this summer. Duluth and surrounding communities were flooded; Duluth is on a hill. We'll see how the fall goes, but in true Minnesotan thinking, I'm sure we are in for record snowfalls and record-setting, sub-zero temperatures this winter.

3] I was driving through Aitkin, Minnesota this morning, and a stretch Escalade limousine was pulling out of the parking lot of a canoe outfitter. That is just wrong!

4] I saw a bumper sticker on the back of a pick-up truck today that read: "My Labrador is Smarter than Your Honor Student!" I don't know if this is a testimony to dog trainers or our American education system.

5] I grew up the son of a career Navy man and lived on or near Navy bases until I was 16 years old, so this has always confused me. We have several stores in Minnesota with names like Fleet Supply, Fleet Farm and L&M Fleet Supply. None of them sell anything Naval related, but New York City hosts Fleet week every year when the sailors are in port.

6] A few weeks ago my friend Steve and I drove to Omaha, Nebraska for the College World Series. We were driving west on I-80 between Des Moines, Iowa and Omaha and were passed by the *American Pickers* van. Both of us are fans of the show, so we chased after it to see if Mike and Frank were driving. We eventually caught up to the van and pulled up alongside of them to take pictures. To our dismay, it was not Mike and Frank. It was the van from the show. This left me wondering if they really drive the van around the country doing picks. I also gained a little perspective of the ups and downs members of the paparazzi must experience.

7] I saw on the news tonight that a recently-released national study found that the average I.Q. score of women in the United States has surpassed that of men for the first time. I hope there wasn't a lot of money spent on this study because these findings have been obvious to me for years.

7/17/2012

8] I had a great Non-Facebook experience today. I was in Morris, Minnesota this week, directing a volleyball camp. I had the pleasure of having dinner tonight with Scott and Lisa Monson. Scott and Lisa were student-athletes of mine in Lake Park, Minnesota in the early 1980s. Scott is now the Superintendent of Morris Public Schools, and Lisa teaches in a small town north of Morris. I haven't seen either one of them in several years. I can't begin to tell you how enjoyable it was to catch up on our lives and old times. When I experience moments like these, I'm always glad I'm not on Facebook and other social networks. I enjoy catching up personally every once in a while, as opposed to the constant daily updates.

9] My wife and I were able to meet our son's girlfriend a couple of weeks ago. He brought her home so she could see his hometown and meet us. They have been dating for 8 months — that is by far a record for Blaine. Pam and I both thought Alex was a very nice young lady, and they make a great couple. Blaine is 27 years old and a sworn bachelor. I think he is closer to going down than he has ever been. We'll see!

7/28/2012

10] I watched the opening ceremony for the 2012 Olympics last night; how great was that? I don't know if that was the largest live audience Paul McCartney has played in front of, but if not if it is true that over one billion people watched it on television, that had to be the largest broadcast audience he has performed for. Who would ever have thought we would live to see Paul McCartney lead a "Hey Jude" sing-a-long and Queen Elizabeth parachute out of a helicopter with James Bond all in one evening of entertainment.

11] I'm directing another Pacesetter Volleyball camp this week at Lake of the Woods High School in Baudette, Minnesota. Tonight I had another wonderful Non-Facebook moment. I went out to dinner at Ballard's Resort with Jill Olson, the LOW volleyball coach, and ran into John Madsen [Smiley], an old college baseball teammate. Smiley was in town with his wife and some friends for a fishing trip he had won from a Hy-Vee grocery store in Mankato, Minnesota. I haven't seen Smiley for several years, but we quickly caught up. You can't have these special moments if you are constantly updating or checking statuses on social computer networks.

12] I have been watching the Olympics this week every time I get a chance. The Fab Five's gold medal in Women's Gymnastics was great as was Gabby Douglas's overall individual gold. I can't believe the pressure these teenage girls are under. It was great the U.S. took the gold, but you have to wonder how the other teams deal with falling short after all the training they do to prepare for the Olympics.

13] I am enjoying the Olympics, but I miss the Cold War rivalries that use to be part of the political mix of the Olympics. It is just not as big a deal anymore when we defeat the Russians. I'm not going to lie; when I watch the women's swimming events I honestly miss the East Germans also.

8/21/2012

14] When I go to the Super One Grocery Store, I often shop at the meat counter. They usually are selling a variety of fresh fish that are advertised as "farm grown." I've never been to a fish farm, so I'm left to wonder: do they plant them with the heads or the tails in the ground, or are they grown from seeds?

15] The women's volleyball team I coach at Hibbing CC has been practicing for a little over two weeks now. We start the regular season in three days. Potentially, we look like a team that could make post-season play. I would feel a lot more comfortable if we started passing better. Things always go better when a team passes well.

16] We took our first extended volleyball trip today. It was a two-hour trip to Brainerd for a women's volleyball scrimmage. We played well and are showing a lot of improvement. I'm especially happy, also, because we did not have to stop once for anyone to pee on the way there or home again. Like I said before, this team has potential. We have a four-hour trip on Friday, so we'll see how that goes.

8/24/2012

17] On Jason Mraz's "Love" CD, the lyrics in the song 5/6 include a line that says, "The world is a reflection of how children play." Try comparing this concept to politics, war, or inter-personal relationships; I see a lot of truth in this.

18] Our volleyball team starts the 2012 volleyball season tomorrow in a tournament at Minnesota State Fergus Falls. We are working on a new mindset. If a player shanks a pass, has a bad set, etc., instead of saying "My bad," they are supposed to say "Fix that," which alerts a teammate to pick them up. Maybe President Obama and the U.S. Congress should try this.

19] The Hibbing CC volleyball team took its annual trip to the Potato Days Festival in Barnesville, Minnesota today. We always go there the day before the Fergus Falls Tournament. The highlight is the Mashed Potato Wrestling Tournament. This year our wrestlers were Jessie LaValley, Laurel Wright, Courtney Wirtanen, and Marina Carter. The ladies were rock stars this year. They got interviewed by the BBC Network and Fox News out of Fargo, North Dakota. I think the Potato Days Festival and Mashed Potato Wrestling takes place the last weekend in August every year in Barnesville, MN. Check it out sometime; it is quite the event.

20] It probably won't happen, but I would like to retire in three years. That will be the end of my 35th year as a teacher and head coach. My wife, Pam, and I discuss future plans every once in a while. Our daughter lives in Auburn, Nebraska with her husband Jeff, and our son lives in Minneapolis, Minnesota. Pam and I live in Hibbing, Minnesota, four hours from Blaine and twelve hours from Lexie and Jeff. It would be nice to live closer to all of them, especially if Lexie and Jeff have kids. Pam and I think they enjoy being able to come home, though. If we moved, we would be living somewhere that wouldn't be home to our kids. Sense of home is important, and it creates an interesting retirement dilemma.

8/25/2012

21] The Fergus Falls volleyball tournament did not go real well today. We lost all four matches. There were some glimmers of brilliance, though, and we'll get back to work next week. I am confident we can "Fix that!"

9/1/2012

22] I am in Minneapolis with my volleyball team for a match with Dakota County Tech. Last night we attended a University of Minnesota volleyball match against Long Island University. Some of my players took notice of the LIU roster, which was loaded with foreign players. They suggested we recruit more foreign players. I told them that we had Magda Chudzik from Poland a couple of years ago. Ironically, within a minute of that conversation, Magda walked down the steps from behind me and sat down to visit. Even though Magda has lived in the Minneapolis area for the last couple of years, how does that happen?

23] We played Dakota County Tech and Gogebic CC today. Played terribly against DCTC and lost in three. The players stepped up in the Gogebic match and won in three sets. Hopefully this will give us a confidence boost going into our first conference match with Vermilion CC on Wednesday night. It is becoming pretty evident we are not a powerful offensive team, so we are going to have to improve our defense and cut down on mistakes in order to be successful. The concept we are trying to bring to volleyball matches is like throwing rocks. We only have a couple of big rocks to throw, so we can't waste them, and in between we have to throw as many little rocks as we can. Eventually something has to hit the floor.

9/2/2012

24] Labor Day weekend Sunday: great day to go fishing. I went to what has become my favorite walleye lake. I say that because I have now caught walleyes the last three times I've been on this lake. Today started out great; I caught two small walleyes within 100 yards of the landing but put them back because I had a feeling that today was going to be better than that. I was right; a little after noon I caught a four-pound walleye and put it on the stringer. If that would have been it, I would have gone home happy and grilled it for dinner. Fifteen minutes later, I hooked into what I was sure was a large northern pike. Turns out it was what I'd estimate to be an eight-pound walleye; biggest one I've ever caught. Two guys that were in another boat about 25 yards away had seen me haul in the two fish and came over to have a look. I proudly hoisted the stringer out of the water and showed the fish off. They wanted to know if I had any walleye tips for them. I have never been asked this question in my life and for good reason. I told them I was mostly fishing with dumb luck, a minnow hooked on a Foxy Jig, and working in about 12 to 14 feet of water just off the weed beds. I was just a "Stupid Man" having the fishing outing of his life, and I reveled briefly in the glory that goes with catching walleyes of that size and giving advice to a couple of guys that wanted to know what my secret was. As it turned out, the advice I should have given is make sure your stringer is attached securely to the boat. About a half hour after holding my fishing clinic, I was making a turn while trolling, and one of the fish jumped and the stringer and the fish sunk out of sight. I spent the remainder of the afternoon trolling and watching for the fish to resurface; no such luck. Somebody found two nice walleyes already on a stringer or there are two nice walleyes caught in the weeds dying a slow death attached to a stringer. I'd like to think someone found them or they at least surfaced and became eagle food. It took me 53 years to catch a walleye that big; I can only hope the next one comes before that. Just to put more salt in the wound, when I got to the boat landing, I went to my truck, got in, and lowered the window. I heard a clunk and the window would not return to the closed position. Hopefully it doesn't rain on the way home. Tomorrow I am going fishing again near Ely, Minnesota, and then I have to put the boat in storage.

9/3/2012

25] Pam and I went to Ely today; she visited with her parents while I went fishing. I stopped at Skube's Bait Shop on the way out of town. They had a 9 ½ pond walleye mounted on the wall. This is how I figured the one I caught yesterday must have been about 8 pounds. The one I caught was 30 inches long, and I had nightmares about it sinking away from the boat that kept me awake all night. It was a beautiful afternoon on the lake, but all I could catch was one northern pike. Nobody was asking for fishing tips today. I broke a tail light loading the boat at the end of the day. That can wait till next spring because the boat went into storage. The day was capped off with a Sir G's Pizza, my personal favorite. Pam and I drove back to Hibbing and stopped to look at a 1968 Cadillac in Tower, MN. Not very practical, but a classic and in great condition. The owners are selling it for $5,000. We are thinking about it.

9/4/2012

26] Big week this week. We have our home opener for volleyball on Wednesday night. Tonight is our first open gym for women's basketball. I start my first year directing intramurals on Thursday. We travel to Rochester, MN for a volleyball tournament this weekend, and I have to complete my annual fall task of finding the Entertainment Weekly Fall TV Preview magazine for my wife. No complaints here; whatever makes her happy. I brought my truck to Northwood's Ford today. Hopefully they can fix my window, and I also asked them to try to get the squeal out of my brakes.

27] I visited with some of our guests at breakfast today. Pam and I own the Mitchell-Tappan House Bed and Breakfast in Hibbing, MN. One of the guests, Kip Johnson, was having a particularly proud moment. Kip was showing off his picture in the Hibbing Daily Tribune; he won the Northwest Open Golf Tournament Super Senior Division. Kip won last year also, but he was cut off in the picture in the paper. This year he positioned himself right in the middle. Kip, originally from Hibbing, comes up almost every year from Florida to play in the tournament.

9/6/2012

28] I was able to pick up my truck today. I brought it to the shop the other day to get the window motor fixed on the driver's side. I also asked them to check the squeal in my front brakes and figure out why my emergency brake light kept coming on and tripping out my cruise control. I ended up with a new window motor and new brake rotors, and it turns out I had busted front springs and struts that needed to be replaced. $1,537.01 later, I drove my truck home. Don't have to worry about buying that Cadillac now. Feels like a whole new truck. Good news: we beat Vermilion in volleyball last night 3-0 and are leaving for Rochester, MN today.

9/7/2012

29] My volleyball team and I are in Rochester today for a game with Rochester tonight. We got into town last night, so we have lots of time for homework before we go to the gym. I have my lecture notes ready for next week's classes, so I'm going to Barnes & Noble to find the Entertainment Weekly Fall Television Preview for my wife.

9/12/2012

30] Really, I love my life; every day presents new challenges. We are preparing to play two conference volleyball matches this weekend. This morning, one of our best players was in a car accident. Thank God she was not seriously injured. She will be missing from the line-up this weekend, though. We have two days to try to figure out how to adjust and cover for her absence.

I just got home from practice, pulled into the garage, and ended the day with a bang. My wife had been working on an old window, stripping paint off of it. The window was in sawhorses in my garage stall. Long story short, I didn't see it and ran over the window and busted most of the glass out of it. Pam heard the crash and came running out of the house to see what the noise was. To say the least, she was upset. Based on the expletives, you would think I did it on purpose. Convinced she thought I did it on purpose, I asked her to consider the alternatives: I did see the window and I ran it over on purpose or, like I said, I never saw the window. My thought was that she could have called and given me a heads up. Most likely I would have forgotten anyway and ran over the window. I am definitely pre-occupied with how to fix our line-up without our injured player. Either way, I am going to quietly eat my dinner, which I'm late for, and go hide in the basement the rest of the night.

9/14/2012

31] I had to go to the drive-thru at the bank today to cash a check. I pulled up and all the lanes were full. I was the only car waiting to take a lane. I never seem to be able to pick the lane that will be available next. I always study the situation and look for who is in the banking process or still waiting. Seems like I always pick the lane where you end up waiting the longest and about the time you decide to back-up and move to an open lane, someone pulls up behind you and you are stuck waiting. I take consolation in the fact that anyone that pulls up behind me is going to wait twice as long as I did, because I always double check receipts if I am depositing, and count the money if I have cashed a check.

32] Same trip to the bank: While sitting there waiting my turn, I overheard the conversation between the teller and a customer. They were lamenting over their separate, single-parent dilemmas. The teller, a male, was upset because his ex-wife won't let him help more with the kids. The customer, a female, was lamenting that her ex-husband had moved to Texas and wanted to have nothing to do with the kids. I hope these two get the chance to visit some more; they could be a good match for each other.

33] I had another Ozone treatment for my Rheumatoid Arthritis today. I had my hip injected and for the second time had blood removed and mixed with the Ozone and Saline and put back into my body. I've been treated at least six times now either injected or received a transfusion. So far, I'd say it is working well. More people should look into Ozone Therapy; it can help treat a lot of different ailments.

34] We had a Volleyball match at Itasca CC. Despite having a new line-up and missing a key player, I thought we played okay even though we lost. Hopefully tomorrow's match at Fond du Lac goes better.

35] I mentioned earlier that I had my truck into the shop for some repairs just last week. One of the repairs was on my driver's side window. Tonight, when I got back from Itasca, I discovered my passenger side window now does not function and it is open. Hopefully I can get it in on Monday and it doesn't rain before then. Lord knows I don't want to have to pull into my garage stall too soon.

9/15/2012

36] Great day; we won our volleyball match at Fond du Lac. We ate at Gordy's Hi-Hat in Cloquet, MN after the match. Gordy's is closing for the season in nine days, so if you aren't going through Cloquet anytime soon you'll have to wait until the spring. It didn't rain and shouldn't the rest of the weekend, so I will not have to park in the garage.

9/17/2012

37] Another great day! Our injured volleyball player got cleared to resume playing. My truck door is fixed; it was a switch not a motor this time around. I supervised co-ed intramurals today at 3:00 p.m. The game was Kitten ball [played with an oversized softball]. Eight students showed up. The weather was fine, so it leads me to wonder, why would a person not want to get out of their dorm room and participate? Last week we had a kick ball game and three students showed up. It was 80 degrees and sunny out. Next week the game is flag football; we'll see how that goes. Maybe I should just wait for the next really nice day and schedule an indoor Madden Video Game Tournament and see how that goes.

38] I haven't quite decided who I'm going to vote for in the Presidential election, but I do know I've never had to choose, pick, or select between two people for anything with the names Barack and Mitt. I am just getting used to Barack conjuring up the image of President in my mind, but I'm having a hard time getting a grip on Mitt. So far all that comes to mind when I hear

Mitt is a poodle. If I was invited to have a beer on the White House lawn, I would prefer that be with President Obama.

9/26/2012

39] I still can't really believe this, but my publisher scheduled me for my first book signing event for *Random Thoughts of a Stupid Man*. I am going to hopefully sell and sign a few books at the Island Book Store on Mackinac Island in Michigan. Pam and I are going to take a long weekend and spend a few days on the island. I never thought this author stuff would be so exciting.

40] The buzz is definitely out there on the replacement referees in the NFL. Being somewhat of a Vikings fan, I don't think the call should have been reversed, either. On the other hand, I do hope they get the real referees back to work soon before some crazed fan gets after one of these guys. It might have got real ugly if that Packers game would have been played in Green Bay instead of Seattle.

41] I talked to my daughter last night. Now that she is not coaching, she doesn't call me much anymore. It is usually her mother she wants to talk to. Apparently, I don't know how to get pregnant, redecorate the house, or want to discuss weddings attended or television shows watched.

42] Yesterday in the Psychology of Adjustment class I teach at the college, I had to add to the discussion we had last week, by my wife's request. Last week we were discussing explanatory style and argumentative goals. I told the class that when my wife and I have an argument/debate, my goal is to end the argument. My wife's goal is to continue until she wins and is right. Pam and I discussed this, and she asked me to revisit this with my class and add that yes, she prefers to win the argument, but she also wants to educate me in the process. I'm not completely sure, but I might be right; just end the argument.

43] No matter what happens today, it is a special day. We are playing Mesabi in volleyball tonight at Mesabi. This is the first Hibbing vs. Mesabi match-up of 2012-2013 other than golf. It is a special rivalry, and win or lose I always look forward to competing with Mesabi no matter what the sport. We are both tied for the fourth and final play-off spot going into tonight's game. We both have seven more games to play after tonight and will face each other one more time. On paper Mesabi appears to be the better squad, but we are convinced we can play with them.

9/27/2012

44] We got beat in three sets in volleyball at Mesabi last night. We weren't very competitive. It always stings a little more when you lose a rival match. I went home feeling terrible and sat out on the porch to stew for a while and absorb it. I turned on ESPN, comfort television, and watched an E:60 episode. The story was about Ben Petrick, the ex- Colorado Rocky who had his career cut short by Parkinson's disease. I found the story very inspiring. It was about his battle with the disease and how he is just trying to be a good father and husband. It was gut-wrenching and definitely helped me put something as insignificant as losing a volleyball match in perspective.

45] Mystery solved! Yesterday I set my watch alarm for 3:30 so I could take a nap before leaving for our volleyball match. The alarm never went off, but I did wake up on time. This morning when I woke up, my wife had just finished showering and was not in a very good mood. Her displeasure was directed at me; apparently my watch alarm went off at 3:30 a.m. and again, as it is designed to do, at 3:35 a.m. She was unable to get back to sleep and, just to throw more fuel on the fire, I never even heard it and continued to sleep soundly. I have to admit, if I don't have my reading glasses on, I don't always get that a.m./p.m. set correctly on my watch.

46] While reading the sports section in the paper this morning, my attention was drawn to two headlines: one was tough to stomach and the other was long overdue. The first one read: "Norsewomen Breeze Past Cardinals, 3-0." The second read: "The NFL and Referees Settle on New Contract."

9/29/2012
12:21A·M· CST

47] I'm sitting here at a hotel room desk in Wahpeton, North Dakota; just shut off my cell phone. Normally I never have my cell phone on this late. I usually shut it off about 10:00 p.m. at the latest. Tonight was different.

My volleyball team played in the NDSCS Tournament today. We lost both matches, but I have to admit we are getting tougher. Despite losing both matches, the ladies were warriors today. We started out with seven players today. We normally have nine. We left Laurel Wright home in Hibbing to attend nursing classes, and Ashley O'Hearon sprained her ankle before we left the hotel. I brought the team to a park to work out for a while because we didn't play until 3:00. Ashley sprained her ankle in a freshmen vs. sophomores sand volleyball match. The freshmen won, but we lost a sophomore. Remember, I'm still the same "Stupid Man" that wrote the first book. To add to the adversity, our lead middle hitter, Jessie LaValley, went down late in the second match. With most remaining players assuming new roles, we battled hard and came up short. I really hope they can step up and have at it again later today [Saturday]. I hope they know I'm proud of them. I'll try to remember to tell them at breakfast.

Back to why my cell phone didn't get shut off till after midnight. My daughter, Lexie, called about 9:30 to let me know my first book, *Random Thoughts of a Stupid Man*, was posted for sale on Amazon. Jenna Massingill, one of my players, showed it to me on her computer. I still can't believe it!

I called my wife to check-in and then went on to call my son, Blaine. After that I began to shamelessly promote the impending release of the book. I called my sisters, a few friends, and ex-players. After finishing talking to Scott Monson, I checked my voicemail and text messages. Apparently there are still people in my life that don't realize I don't text. I do read text messages and delete them immediately. The messages ranged from shock to congratulations! Either way, I'm thankful to anyone who is promoting or buying the book. Special shout out to Hunter Naisbitt, an ex-player who is serving as an unofficial publicist.

I have to finish writing a test for my Psychology of Adjustment class and try to get some sleep. This whole "Author/Stupid Man" thing is stressing me out. I've been freezing for the past half hour now and I just figured it out. The window is open, the air conditioner is on, and I'm in Wahpeton, ND and it is 12:45

a.m. on September 29th. I'll go make sure my players locked their doors and they are sleeping, then I'll hit my knees and thank God for another great day!

10/4/2012

48] We have six more matches left in our conference volleyball season. Currently we are still on the hunt for the fourth and final spot in the region volleyball tournament. We also have the possibility of having to play a play-off game with Mesabi Range CC the weekend of October 19th. My wife and I are planning to go to Mackinac Island in Michigan that weekend, and I have my first book signing for *Random Thoughts of a Stupid Man* at the Island Book Store on October 19th because that is our fall break at the college and we have a four-day weekend. If we get a play-off game, I won't go on the trip, but hopefully Pam can go; she needs a break from running the Bed & Breakfast. She can sign books as "The Wife of a Stupid Man."

Pam would like to make reservations for our stay, but it is hard to do so if you don't know when the volleyball season will end. This is the usual process for Pam and me when planning a vacation. We usually can't solidify plans in advance because of the uncertainty of when a sports season might end. Basically, the better the season, the shorter the vacation. It is not easy having your life put on hold by eighteen- and nineteen-year-old, college women; it's harder the longer my coaching career goes on.

Technically we are "empty-nesters," but between guests at our Bed & Breakfast and me still coaching two sports, you would never know it.

10/11/2012
THURSDAY

49] My daughter called to tell my wife she is taking a pregnancy test on Sunday. I know we would love to be grandparents and Lexie and Jeff are trying to have a baby, but is this update really necessary? Either way, I'm looking forward to the call on Sunday.

50] We lost to Mesabi last night in volleyball. Played well, but there were too many unenforced errors to win it; pretty much the story of the 2012 season. We are now one loss away from not being able to make the region tournament or Pam making our reservations for Makinac Island, depending on how you look at it. It amazes me sometimes how twelve missed serves and ten attack errors can actually alter the direction my life takes.

10/25/2012

51] Pam and I got back from our Mackinac Island trip on Sunday night. I'm not going to lie; I'm disappointed the volleyball season is over, but the trip was great. We left on Wednesday afternoon and did a quick stop in Bayfield, Wisconsin. We shopped around a little, went to an orchard, and then stopped at a winery—Hauser's Farm—picked up a few bottles, and went on to Ashland, WI. We stayed at a Bed & Breakfast there, Inn at Timber Cove, and went out to eat at Platters. I had prime rib, and Pam had the whitefish. I threw that tidbit in there because my mother-in-law always wants to know what we ate when we go out to eat. The next day we went a little further across the Upper Peninsula and stopped at another B&B. We did do a quick stop in Marquette, MI, shopped around, and did a quick tour of the field house on the University of Northern Michigan campus. That is an amazing structure. My wife is not much of a sports fan but even she had to admit it was pretty cool. Between the field house and Mackinac Island, the trip across the Upper Peninsula was definitely worth the otherwise boring drive. Along the way, I asked several people why the Upper Peninsula is even included in Michigan's boundaries. Even people in Michigan seemed to agree it should be part of Wisconsin.

Mackinac Island was fantastic—one might even say "Grand." We took the ferry from St. Ignace to the island. First we walked the main street and the shops, had a quick lunch at the Pink Pony, and then walked up the hill to check in at the Grand Hotel. I was supposed to do a book signing at the Island Bookstore but was unable to because my books couldn't be shipped in time. We had dinner that night at the hotel. Not exactly my style—you had to wear a suit and tie—but the dinner was great.

Eventually I got over the suit and tie thing, but I still was uncomfortable with the waiter placing my napkin in my lap. After dinner we went to a showing of *Somewhere in Time*, a Christopher Reed movie that had been filmed at the Grand Hotel. Afterwards we went to one of the ballrooms and danced to some Big Band music. I'm not much for dancing, but I did have a suit and tie on, and I love Big Band music.

The next day was a whirlwind. We had breakfast at the hotel, took a horse-carriage tour of the Island, and then rented bikes and did a 57-minute cruise around the island before catching the ferry at 3:00. On the way home, we stopped and stayed at Chamberlin's Ole Forest Inn in Curtis, MI. We sat at the bar and watched the second half of the Michigan vs. Michigan State football game and acted like locals. We met a couple from Wisconsin and had a great time at dinner with them. Other than being excited about Wisconsin beating Minnesota that day, Bob and Mary were great to hang out with. We had breakfast the next day with them before heading home.

52] Yesterday was just great. It was Wednesday and that is my shot day—I give myself an Embrel shot for my Rhuematoid Arthritis. I also had an 8:00 a.m. dentist appointment to get a crown put on. The dentist did not like the condition the tooth was in, so we opted to pull it. I managed to drool and slur my way through several meetings during the day. Basketball practice went well, and then I went recruiting for volleyball. When I returned home that night I found out Cassie, the doctor who gives me my Ozone therapy, was in town and had time to do an Ozone blood infusion. I think the ozone therapy is working and Cassie only comes around so often, so we did the infusion. After the infusion I was playing with the idea of having a beer but found out that our German guests at our Bed & Breakfast had already drank my beer.

53] Winter may have officially arrived today. I had to shovel snow this morning. I like shoveling, but it is only October 25th. Jody, one of our regular guests from Louisville, Kentucky was very excited and took pictures to send home to the nonbelievers. When I got to the college, I was treated to another fantastic Non-Facebook moment. A sales representative came to my office. It was Ron Dabill. Ron is working for 2nd Wind Exercise Equipment out of Lindstrom, MN. Ron played basketball for me in Wadena in 1989. 1992 was probably the last time I had seen him or heard from him. It was great catching up and hearing how his life has turned out so far. I told him about my first book, Random Thought of a Stupid Man, and he plans to buy one. He gets it; he is married and has three daughters, two in high school. He is pretty sure he has been called a "Stupid Man" also. I love running into ex-players and students and re-connecting. It is a heart-warming experience, especially when you find out that they are doing well.

10/31/2012

54] Now the Jersey Shore has a real "Situation." Watching the aftermath of Hurricane Sandy on the news is devastating. I am thankful that I have never had to personally deal with a natural disaster that even remotely compares to what the people up and down the east coast are dealing with. I don't have enough money to send out that way for disaster relief, nor can I travel out east anytime soon to try and help. I can pray for the well-being of all those involved, though.

55] The toughest job in the country right now, besides being a single mom, has to be being President Obama's campaign advisor. I see he has to step off the campaign trail to assess the Hurricane damage on the east coast, while Romney, on the other hand, can continue to campaign. I'm sure a lot of voters will react both ways to this. Some will think he is returning to campaigning too soon and has bigger things to worry about. Many of these same people will probably be the same people upset if the National Football League doesn't play any games scheduled on the east coast this week. Romney sure as hell better not even attempt to blame President Obama for any lost stock market activity, job loss, or gas price hikes incurred because of Hurricane Sandy. It will be very interesting to see how this plays out for both can-didates.

56] I'm not complaining, but I'm tired. We have had basketball practice every night this week and a 6:15 a.m. practice on Tues-day. I went to Bemidji last night and Duluth tonight to recruit players for next year's volleyball team. Tomorrow night we have our first basketball scrimmage at Vermilion, practice on Friday, and Saturday I'm going back to Duluth to watch and hopefully talk to more prospective volleyball players. Recruiting was a lot easier when I was old enough to be an older brother of the prospects. Then I was old enough to be their dad. Now, in some cases, I could be their grandpa. I can only hope that I don't come off as a scary, old man when I first meet recruits. If they can get past that and come to Hibbing Community College, they find out I'm a good guy to play for and they can definitely get a quality education here. I will admit, though, I can be a little scary if we are having a bad night in practice.

11/25/2012

57] Not that I haven't been thinking lately, I just haven't found the time to write some of these thoughts down.

58] We started practicing for the 2012-2013 basketball season on October 1st. We opened our season on November 9th & 10th in Mason City, Iowa against Ellsworth CC and North Iowa Area CC. To say the least, we got pounded. Tough opening weekend against two very good teams, both NJCAA Division ll teams — we are a Division lll team. The difference being they have athletic scholarships and we don't. It was possibly an ill-advised way to open the season with the inexperienced, young team we have this year. I still cling to the concept of playing tough opponents to get tougher. We'll see how it plays out this year.

59] Twinkies, Suzy Q's, and Ho Ho's were three of my favorite, childhood snacks. I still sneak a Suzy Q every once in a while. With Hostess going bankrupt and liquidating, I hope someone buys the recipes and continues production. Little Debbies just don't cut it all the time.

60] Possibly, Alabama and Notre Dame are in the NCAA football title game. How cool is that?

61] I received an e-mail from Amazon today, canceling an order. It was a non-responsive e-mail, which obviously can't be responded to. It would be nice to know why the order was canceled. They did send me a survey to fill out pertaining to what I thought about their service. What is the point, if I can't find out why my order was cancelled?

62] I just caught a highlight on Sports Center. If I wait twenty minutes, I should be able to catch it again. I want to make sure what I thought I saw was true. I understand Ohio State honoring their 2002 football team, but why Coach Tressel? Didn't they fire him last year? I have coached for thirty-two years. If I ever am a part of putting one of my teams on probation, I wouldn't expect that school to honor me. I might end my career leaving a gym feet first, but I doubt I'll be on anyone's shoulders, and if I am, I hope I have a national championship trophy in my hands. Most likely, though, I'll be on a gurney with a sheet over my head.

63] Before the next Presidential election, the Republicans should review the rules on Monopoly. You can have all the Indiana Avenues you want. You need to win Boardwalk and Park Avenue to succeed.

64] Wal-Mart employees, upset with the stores for opening early on Thanksgiving and cutting into family time, stood in protest lines on Thanksgiving, protesting not being able to be with their families. I'm not sure, but it had to be tough to find time for Thanksgiving dinner between protesting and working.

65] I'll admit it, I participated in Black Friday. My son Blaine and I went to the Brandon Tree Farm north of Nashwauk, MN to cut a Christmas tree. It was crazy; traffic was stopped for two minutes on County Road 8 because of an accident. Traffic was backed up four cars deep. When we got to the tree farm, there were at least three other people looking for trees. Later in the day, it was even more stressful when I went to L&M Supply to pick-up sidewalk salt. All four tills were open and at least two people were in each line. There was a huge Carhart display right in the main entry, and they were out of 10-pound bags of salt. I had to buy a 50-pound bag. I know I'll have to go back to the tree farm next year, but I think I'll buy salt the Wednesday before Thanksgiving, just to avoid the rush.

66] Thanksgiving was nice this year; my sister Stacie and her family hosted for the first time. They did a great job! My daughter Lexie and her husband Jeff came up from Nebraska, and Blaine brought his girlfriend Alex. My sister Terri was sick and couldn't attend. Everything went well, except my mom made a big speech about how proud she was of her kids and grandchildren and sons- and daughters in-law. She said she wanted to say that in case this was her last Thanksgiving. Pretty much put everyone to tears. I'm sure she is going to be around for several more, but I pray there isn't something she isn't telling us.

12/2/2012

67] I'm hiding in my office at school. Today is the second day of the Christmas Tea & Boutique at the Mitchell-Tappan House Bed and Breakfast. My wife and her friends Mary and Roz have been hosting this for eight years now. It gets bigger every year. They have several other women that come in and help during the two-day event. Close to 300 people come to the house, have tea and lunch, then tour the house and shop the ornaments. Those people, mostly women, seem to enjoy it immensely. Pam, Mary, and Roz begin decorating the house in October and seem to stress out more every year. I don't know how many years they can keep it up. My goal every year is the same. I help with whatever they want leading up to the event, and then try to be as scarce as I can the days of the tea. So far it is working for me.

68] My basketball team had two games this past weekend. We lost by 36 and 39 points. I know this may be hard to believe, but I think we are showing signs of improvement. Slow but sure, but we are starting to figure a few things out. I hope this continues; we have a month and a half before we start conference play.

69] One of my back-up freshman guards came to me after Saturday's game to tell me she has to stop playing basketball. She has to drop her chemistry class, which will put her under 12 credits, making her ineligible. She does plan to be in school next semester but thinks she only has to take a few business courses and doesn't feel she has to worry about getting a degree anymore. She is purchasing a building in a small, northern Minnesota town and starting an online auction store. She hopes to parlay that into her own grocery store sometime in the future. I hope she is a lot smarter than me and this all works out for her, because right now, I'm just not seeing it. All I know as of now: I have nine players and fall semester ends in two weeks. I hope everyone else makes grades, because we need every one of those women the rest of the season. I'm recruiting my butt off, but that is for next season.

70] Just had another one of those great Non-Facebook moments. Shaun Ballard called because he had heard about my first book, *Random Thoughts of a Stupid Man*. We talked for quite a while and caught up. Shaun played men's basketball for me here at Hibbing CC about twelve years ago. He came to us from Columbus, Ohio, then went on to play at Northland College in Ashland, WI and completed an elementary education degree. Presently, he is living in Columbus, is the co-owner of three pizza shops, and works at a Recreation Center. It still always warms my heart to hear from past student-athletes, especially when things are going well. Shaun was a kid that came here without any inkling of what he wanted to do other than play basketball and somehow found his way to using the opportunity to make something good happen for himself. Maybe I should share this story with the girl that quit yesterday.

71] After I got home from our game last night, I watched Alabama beat Georgia in the SEC Football Championship game. I am real excited about the thought of Alabama and Notre Dame playing for the National Championship. In the morning I watched Nick Saban's, Alabama's coach, press conference. At one point he said everyone talks about being defined by the moment and how he thought it was much more important for an athlete to define the moment. All I could think of was that line from Dead Poets Society, "Seize the Day!" Either way, I love the mindset. "Roll tide!"

12/5/2012

72] I was thinking about Steve Hucke this morning; kind of hard not to. Steve is the baseball and women's basketball coach at Rochester Community and Technical College in Rochester, MN. Steve and I go way back, but that is not why he is in my thoughts. Steve called me the other night to tell me they left their blue uniforms at Itasca CC this past weekend. Normally, not something I would get involved in, but it just so happens that we are playing at Rochester this Saturday. So between Steve, me, and Justin Lampaa, the Athletic Director at Itasca, we figured how to get the uniforms here so I can take them to Rochester on Saturday. Not bad for three "Stupid Men"! The uniforms were dropped off at my office this morning, and I washed them and bagged them up. Hopefully I'll remember to put them on the bus this weekend. I'm not sure how Saturday's game will go, but you'd think Rochester would owe us one! Do you think Bobby Knight ever washed an opponent's uniforms? Just another reminder that I'm living the dream! I called Steve this morning to let him know I had the uniforms and would be bringing them. He was home, sick; like I could care. The sad thing was he had one of his best players go down with an ACL tear in a game last night. This is always upsetting, whether it happens to one of your own players or that of an opponent. I still have not figured out why knee injuries seem so common in women's athletics. I have my theories, but no real answers. It is just sad to see it happen. Our players receive no athletic scholarships and most are playing strictly because of a love of the game. There just doesn't seem to be any fairness when you see them go down with a major injury. I know there are risks to participating in athletics, but that doesn't make it any easier.

Steve and I and our baseball teams shared a tragic moment in Rochester a few years ago. A couple of innings into a game, one of his outfielders collapsed on the field with an apparent heart problem. EMTs were called to the field and worked on the kid for quite a while. He was pronounced dead at one point, before later being revived. He was brought to the hospital and ended up regaining his health. The whole time the EMTs were working to save the kid, our baseball teams knelt on the infield hand in hand, praying and consoling each other. Anyone who has ever worked with eighteen- to twenty-year-old, young men knows this was a special moment. I'll never forget it, and I know those players or anyone at that game won't, either.

73] On a lighter note: My first book, Random Thoughts of a Stupid Man, has been for sale for a couple of months now. I have received some good reviews from people who have read it. I'm sure there are those who didn't like it, but I haven't talked to them yet. People keep asking me why I didn't tell this story or that story in the first book. Thinking of Steve Hucke, one came to mind. I know this is not the story he wants me to tell, but if that story is going to be told, he will have to write his own book.

Three summers ago I was on my way to Saint Cloud, MN to work at the Pacesetter Top 100 Basketball Show Case. When I arrived at the Holiday Inn to check-in, I met Steve in the parking lot. When I got out of my truck, I knelt down and started looking under the truck. Steve asked what was wrong. I stood up and told him I had hit a pig on the trip from Hibbing to Saint Cloud. I came up over a hill, and there were a bunch of pigs in the road, and I hit and killed one. I felt terrible! I got out of my truck and stood there, not knowing what to do. There were no houses in sight and nobody drove by to check on me or the pigs. The rest of the pigs just stood there and stared at me; it was kind of creepy. I did notice a break in the fence and figured that must be where the pigs got out of the field. I told Steve it had been several minutes now, and I still had not seen anyone, it was just me one dead pig and the others standing alongside the road staring at me. I decided just to pull the dead pig off the road and continue my drive to Saint Cloud. I still felt weird about it. It wasn't like it was a deer or some other wild animal.

By now, Steve had crawled under my truck to take a look for himself. I went on to tell him that wasn't the end of the story. I was pulled over by a Sheriff outside of Ogilvie, MN. He asked if I had been traveling near Isle, MN about a ½ hour ago. I said yes. He issued mea ticket for $500 for leaving the scene of an agricultural accident. He said I could mail in the fine or show up in court and challenge the ticket. Steve popped out from under the truck, bewildered. He said, "I thought you said nobody was around?" I said, "I know; no houses, no barn, and nobody drove by." Steve asked me if the Sheriff said why he knew it was me. I said he did. Steve asked again, "What did he say?" My response: "He said one of the pigs squealed!" Steve was irate that I had suckered him in. Steve is originally from Iowa; you'd think he could see a pig joke coming right away!

12/10/2012

74] I don't know if this fits into the stupid category or what; you can be the judge. This past weekend we traveled to LaCrosse, Wisconsin and Rochester, MN for basketball games on Friday and Saturday. We got kicked around pretty good in Friday's game and took an eleven-point lead into halftime before eventually losing to Rochester by ten. Our 8th and 9th losses of the season, but we are getting better and I hope we'll be competitive in our own division. We arrived home about midnight on Saturday.

On Sunday I left at 6:30 a.m. to drive down to Minneapolis to go to the Vikings vs. Bears game with my son. Paid way too much for the tickets from Stub Hub, but oh, well. The drive took the normal four hours. The game was great; the Vikes won, and I got to spend some quality time with Blaine and saw his new condominium downtown. During the day, Minneapolis got 14 inches of snow — fortunately not enough to take down the stadium roof again. I decided to drive home after the game. I left at 4:30 and arrived in Hibbing after midnight. The trip ended up taking about twice as long as normal. This morning, I spent three hours shoveling and snow blowing before going to school. Tonight I have to go recruiting.

I am not a passionate Vikings fan, so it leaves me to wonder if it was all worth it. I did see a great game, and any time I get to spend with either one of my kids these days is priceless. I'm going with: it was all worth it!

12/19/2012

75] I had to go to the clinic today and do a blood work-up in the Lab. I'm supposed to have a lab done every six months for my Rheumatoid Arthritis. Apparently, I missed a lab appointment on November 16th. I found this out because my wife called to refill my Embrel prescription and the pharmacist couldn't because they had been informed by my doctor's office that I had missed a lab and they wouldn't sign off until I had a lab test done. I'm left to wonder why my doctor didn't give me a heads up on missing the lab test. I'm glad my pharmacist is looking out for me, but I would feel better if my doctor's office would show a little more concern for my well-being. Preventative medicine?

76] Prayers for all those involved in any way with the Sandy Hook Elementary School shooting.

12/21/2012

77] Just wanted to write something to bear witness to the fact that, despite the Mayan Calendar running out, the world did not end today. I'm sure of this because it snowed last night and I had to shovel this morning. Actually, it has turned out okay today; first sub-zero temperatures of the year, but that was bound to happen.

I received some good news and bad news today. Good news: the world did not end today and 9 out of 10 of my basketball players are academically eligible for the second semester. Bad news: I lost my top rebounder and second leading scorer to fall semester grades. I will deal with that next week. Right now all that matters is Christmas is just three days away, my son is coming home tonight, and my daughter and son-in-law will be home tomorrow night. A huge snowstorm hit Iowa, which they have to drive through. Hopefully all goes well as they travel up here. Prayers for all those traveling over the Holidays, and special thoughts and prayers for those families that lost children or other loved ones in the Sandy Hook shootings, as they attempt to cope with the grief during the holidays and the coming New Year.

12/27/2012

78] I have always been a believer, and Christmas is by far my favorite holiday. The spirit of Christmas has definitely been challenged this year, with tragedies such as Hurricane Sandy, Sandy Hook, and the guy outside of Rochester, New York trying to burn down his neighborhood, killing his sister, and two firefighters, just to name a few. Despite all this, Christmas came and went all over the world, and people celebrated the birth of Christ. I hope everyone was able to gain some sense of peace, joy, and hope from the spirit of Christmas, even if only a brief reprieve from troubled times.

79] My daughter Lexie, her husband Jeff, their dog Daisy, and my son Blaine all left yesterday, after spending a few days home for Christmas. Blaine's girlfriend Alex could not make it; hopefully she can next year. It was great having everyone home for Christmas. We went up to Ely for a couple of days and the Loes and LaTourells had everyone home also, so it was a special year. It has been a few years since my side of the family has come up over the holidays; I really hope it works out with everyone's schedules sometime soon.

Pam and I both love our children dearly and are excited anytime they come home. I'm not going to lie though, despite how well Pam always decorates for Christmas, the best lights are the headlights of our kid's cars when they come home and their taillights when they leave.

12/28/2012

80] Congratulations to Anders Broman of Lakeview Christian Academy out of Duluth. Anders is an outstanding player on the LCA boys' basketball team. Last night he scored 42 points against Mesabi East High School. The 42 points was no big deal for him; the special part of this was that put him at 4,122 points for his career. This is a new, Minnesota high school record which was previously held by Kevin Noreen of Minnesota Transitions High School. The old record, set in 2010, was 4,086 points.

Anders is well deserving of any accolades he gets. He seems to be a kid of quality character and works very hard at his craft. By all indications, he is a good student, outstanding leader, and professes his Christian faith openly. He plays a very unselfish game, and his teammates seem to respect him. He is a senior and it is early in the season, so who knows where he will leave the record when he is done.

1/4/2013

81] I may have said this before, but I am a peanut butter fanatic. To say the least, peanut butter has been a staple food for me since I was young. My mom always served Skippy. After getting married I made the switch to Jif. As I recall, this is also when I switched from Hellman's Mayonaise to Kraft Miracle Whip. It wasn't just because I got married; Pam had been raised on Jif and Miracle Whip and she was buying the groceries.

Today I heard on the radio and read in the newspaper that Hormel was purchasing Skippy Peanut Butter. I'm convinced I am not alone on my love of peanut butter; the purchase price was $700 million dollars! I'm giving serious consideration to buying stock in Jif.

1/7/2013

82] I have had three fantastic Non-Facebook experiences in the last two days. Yesterday, Laura Girard stopped by our house with her boyfriend. Laura attended Hibbing CC and played volleyball for us in 2006 and 2007. I haven't seen her in a couple of years. She was in town for Carrie Kozumplik's wedding— one of her ex-teammates. I had to miss the wedding because of a basketball trip. [Note to self: Send Carrie a present.] It was great to visit with Laura and catch up; always a treat when I hear from her.

Later in the day, Mike Johnson called. Mike is a retired basketball and baseball coach who I had the pleasure of coaching against when he was at Ridgewater CTC in Willmar, MN. He called to tell me he had just finished reading my first book and enjoyed it immensely. His daughter, Carrie Ogdahl, who coaches the women's basketball team at Ridgewater, bought it for him for Christmas. Mike told me that Lowell Roisum, my principal in Wadena, had been a high school classmate of his. He also told me that he almost applied for the Brainerd CC job the year I started there, but his wife talked him out of it. I'm glad that is how it worked out, because he would have got the job because of his bump rights in the MNSCU system. No telling what path my life or his would have taken if he would have taken the job. I think we are both glad it worked out the way it did.

Today I received a letter [a piece of paper with a long message written on it, for those who don't know what one is or haven't seen one in a while] from Rich and Gail Janezich. They enjoyed reading the book also. They pointed out something I hadn't thought about. Rich and Gail grew up in Chisholm, MN. They enjoyed my stories about Ely in the 1970s because all they had to do was change the names of people, streets, lakes, and parks and my story became their story. I think this is why people who have lived here take great pride in saying they are from "The Range," in reference to the Iron Range of northeast Minnesota. Most outsiders don't take much notice to the names of the towns. It doesn't matter if you tell them you are from Ely, Chisholm, Virginia, Keewatin, Buhl, etc., they hear the name of the town and say, "So you are from The Range."

83] I am looking forward to watching Alabama and Notre

Dame play for the BCS National title tonight. Roll Tide!

1/14/2013

84] Note to self: Send Carrie Kozumplik a wedding present.

85] We lost a nonconference basketball game at Gogebic CC in Ironwood, Michigan this past Wednesday night. During the men's game one of our Hibbing players was injured, and I had to go sit in the Emergency Room with him for a few hours. I'm pretty sure this is the sixth or seventh time I've had the pleasure of spending time with a player at the clinic in Ironwood.

While sitting in the lobby and minding my own business, I was somehow drawn into a conversation with two women. One of them was pregnant and thought she was carrying her baby too low after six months. She showed me her belly and asked my opinion. I usually do an okay job of thinking before responding to questions. On this occasion I was thinking to myself, *Do I look like a doctor, and if not, why should I care or have an opinion?* I also had flashbacks of the original Alien movie. That belly was by far the ugliest one I have seen. Lots of veins and stretch marks and something other than a human being was growing in there.

After gathering my thoughts, my response was: "It has been 28 years since I had to pay any attention to a pregnant belly, so I'm really not the guy to ask."

86] Why are so many people up in arms about Brent Musburger's comments during the Alabama and Notre Dame game, pertaining to the Alabama quarterback's girlfriend, who happened to be an ex-Miss Alabama? I don't remember exactly what he said, but he did make reference to her being absolutely gorgeous. Anyone watching that game—male, female, young, old, you name it—thought exactly the same thing. The cameraman obviously thought so, because he came back to her every time he could. Brent needed to talk about something, the game was already out of hand, and Alabama was winning big. Roll tide!

87] A couple more outstanding Non-Facebook moments happened in the past week. Last Thursday I ran into Danielle Zubich at a Chisholm basketball game. When I saw her, it was obvious I hadn't seen her for a while nor do I follow Facebook postings, because Dani is six months pregnant and her and her husband, Chris, are expecting twins. Chris is also a twin. Which leads me to a correction of something I wrote in my first book. I said that Sarah and Dani Ysen were the only twins that I have coached; please add Chris and Tim Zubich to that list. Chris and Tim played baseball here at Hibbing CC in the early 2000s. This year we have Allana and Leigh Lampton playing women's basketball for us, so now I've coached three sets of twins. Still haven't got any better at telling any of them apart unless they are wearing jerseys.

On Saturday we played Central Lakes College. One of my ex-players, Scott Savor, was assisting the men's team. I hadn't seen Scott in fifteen years, so it was a real treat to visit with him. He gave me a copy of a book he has published, *Secrets in Sports*. Scott is a world reknowned trainer and motivational speaker and is very good at what he does. Check him out at www.secretsinsports.com . As I have always said, it is a great feeling when you find out how well someone is doing that you once taught or coached.

After our game on Saturday, Dan Christy stopped by my office to visit. Dan played basketball for me in Hibbing in 2002-2004. Happily married, has an eight month old daughter, lives in Grand Forks, ND, and manages a Red Lobster restaurant. Again, good people doing well!

88] I heard a commercial on the radio today which I've heard a few times now. It distresses me. The commercial is for a national chain of Assisted Living Homes called A Home for Mom. I get it; I'm a Dad, I realize we take a backseat to Mom. This scares me, though; is this place only for elderly widows or does Dad just have to fend for himself? I do hope that I die before my wife, but if I don't, I will pray my children can find at least a tent for Dad.

89] Back to practice today. We are now 0-15 on the year. Great bunch of young ladies, but we are having an extremely difficult time trying to get a win. They are still working at it and I hope having a good time. We did do a lot of things better in two losses over the weekend, and I hope we can keep going forward from there. I really hope we can put 40 good minutes together and pull out a win soon. We have twelve more games.

1/26/2013

90] Very interesting week. Not over yet; it is Saturday morning and we just finished our shoot around. We play Rainy River CC today. I'll get back to that later; I've got to get some things ready for the game.

91] On Sunday, another great Non-Facebook moment occurred in my life. I received a phone call from Brad Griffith. The last time I ever knew of or spoke to Brad was in 1972. He was a friend in the neighborhood in Alameda, California. I was in eighth grade and Brad was in seventh. It wasn't completely out of the blue; my mom and Brad's mom have stayed in touch over the years. The bond between military wives is stronger than any of us will ever realize. His mom had told Brad about my book, and he decided to get in touch.

Brad and I got to talk for a while and plan to do so more in the near future. I did find out he is a building contractor in Sequim, WA, but even more interesting, he is known as the "Worm Guy" because of his knowledge pertaining to night crawlers. Brad is also an expert stick bender. He has been married three times and moved from the Seattle area to Sequim during the Y2K panic. that's something we really didn't experience here in the Midwest, at least not in northeastern Minnesota. I hope to be talking to him again real soon. I'm definitely intrigued.

Pam and I also got to spend the day in Duluth. It is always nice to get away anytime. Between my coaching schedule and her running our Bed & Breakfast, the opportunity to bug out doesn't happen too often. We went to the Zeitgeist downtown and saw *Hyde Park on the Hudson*; great movie! We did a little shopping—yay! Finished up with dinner at the Texas Road-house Grille: cold beer and great steak!

92] On Monday after practice I made a bold decision and decided to let two of our basketball players go. I have been lamenting over this decision for weeks. Despite being 0-16, we have been trying to remain positive and keep working hard at getting better. The most important thing is to respect your teammates and coaches and their contributions to the team and our efforts. These two just wouldn't buy in. So we dropped our roster of nine players to seven for the remainder of the season, eleven more games.

I may have done something right; the mood in practice on Tuesday was 100% better, and the remaining seven players seemed happy with the new arrangement. Wednesday, we were all rewarded with a 72-67 win over Fond Du Lac CC. Down 11 points with four minutes to go, we gutted it out and came back and won, our first win of the year. Usually any big wins you look back on are found in the play-offs. This was just as rewarding as any win I've ever been a part of. It was indescribable to watch the weight of sixteen losses come off everyone's backs.

93] For most of this week we have been experiencing a good, old-fashioned, northern Minnesota winter. Temperatures have been as low as 51 degrees below zero when you factor in the wind chill. We had three days where the daytime temperatures did not get above zero. Our son-in-law Jeff has been following our weather from Nebraska; our daughter Lexie says this is definitely not helping convince him to move to Minnesota. As much as Pam and I would love to have them up here, I don't think it will be happening anytime soon. I don't blame them; I'm always trying to convince Pam that we should move south. How do the global warming enthusiasts explain our coldest winter in years?

94] The other day I was watching some of the Super Bowl hype on ESPN. It was a feature on OJ Brigance, the ex-Raven who is stricken with ALS disease. Stories like this do have a sad note to them but can also be uplifting. During the show, OJ was quoted with saying something I wrote down immediately and was definitely worth sharing: "No matter what we are going through, there is purpose wrapped in the pain."

1/27/2013

95] Refer to Random Thought #92. We lost to Rainy River yesterday by 32 points. The team mood was upbeat afterwards. I asked my players if they were still okay playing with seven players, even though it was obvious we gassed out in the last ten minutes of the game after playing a solid thirty minutes. Their answer was a resounding, unanimous, yes! I like the direction we are moving, and we seem to be united for the first time all year. We'll see how the last eight games of the year turn out.

96] I tried to rewire a new switch in one of our bathrooms today. Luckily nobody is staying in that room tonight. Hopefully the electrician can come bail me out tomorrow. I have never claimed to be a craftsman, but my wife should know by now that electrician and plumber are definitely not even remotely referred to in my 'resume'. I'll stick to groundskeeping.

2/12/2013

97] Coaching and parenting are something I have found to be very similar over the years. I have been parenting for 30 years now and coaching for 32 years. I have been an assistant parent and a head coach during that time. You make a lot of decisions in playing both roles. Hopefully the bottom line is you always have the best interest of the kids in mind. Sometimes you get to see immediately if you made a good or bad choice and other times you need to let it play out over the course of years. There are also times when you know exactly what you are doing and other times you are just flying by the seat of your pants. Either way you have to make decisions and deal with the consequences, good and bad.

I do think we all need to remember, though, that parents don't need to tell coaches how to do their jobs and coaches should refrain from telling parents how to do their jobs. We both have a limited scope of each other and what we do. It's tough to advise anyone unless we know the whole picture, 24/7.

98] Two more Non-Facebook moments. Kelly Hams, an ex-volleyball and basketball player, gave birth to a healthy baby boy last week. Samantha Lindfors, also an ex-player, drove over from Virginia the other day to show me her engagement ring. I'm excited for both of them and wish them all the best.

99] My wife and I and some friends went to a concert at the Hibbing CC theater last night. The performers were Davina and the Vagabonds from Minneapolis/ St. Paul. They are an outstanding Jazz Band and did a great show — very high energy and diverse.

I would have been happy to hear Davina do Etta James covers all night long, but the other songs were great also. I couldn't believe we got that kind of quality performance for a ticket price of $5.00; I would have paid $50.00 and still left happy.

100] This morning I had the pleasure of speaking at the Hibbing Breakfast Rotary meeting. Free breakfast and I had a chance to promote my first book, *Random Thoughts of a Stupid Man*. I guess this means I'm officially on the speaking circuit; not bad considering I don't have an agent.

I passed out a few book promotion cards for the first time. I noticed they say, "The new book" by Mike Turnbull. Good marketing ploy, considering it is also my first book. My wife has already said I can attempt to publish a second book if and when I sell 1,000 copies of the first book. We'll see!

101] Valentine's Day is this Thursday. My wife Pam told me today it is alright for me to go basketball recruiting that night if I want to. We are going to dinner and another concert on Friday. I had planned on staying home on Thursday, but Pam thinks I should go recruit. I really hope this is not a test! Lord knows I need players for next year; we are 1 & 22 on the season right now. That said, I haven't seen any prospects that are worth a divorce.

102] I read an article today discussing Pope Benedict XVI's impending resignation. The article led into talking about people leaving what were once considered lifelong jobs. There was also a discussion of how today's ever-changing world puts an extra strain on elderly people trying to physically, mentally, and emotionally continue to adapt. Considering this information, and even though the resignation is based in health concerns, I am left to wonder if there is a correlation between the Pope's failing health and him opening a Twitter account. He is the first Pope to resign and the first to have a Twitter account. I'm not sure, but he seemed to be okay before he started Tweeting.

103] Very upsetting news this week. One of my good friends and coaching rivals had to resign last Friday with five games left in the regular season. None of us will probably ever know the reasons why, but all I can say is that it is an absolute shame that anything like this has to happen. You spend sixteen years in a position and do it very well, and it all comes to an end and you're asked to clean out your office and turn in your keys; no real explanation and not even a blink. Pretty scary stuff! I'm going to miss competing against him, and I hope something better comes his way.

2/20/2013

104] Another correction from my first book: I had said that the Ysens were the only twins I have coached; since then I have been reminded about the Zubichs and that has been noted in this book. This past weekend I spoke to Dustin Pleshe, and he made me clear on the fact that he and Darin are twins. I have to be granted a pass on this one; they didn't graduate from high school together. I also want to add Allana and Leigh Lampton, who are currently playing on my women's basketball team. They claim to be and are twins but show no signs of any of the stereotypical twin connections.

105] Again, note to self, send off a wedding present to Carrie Kozumplik.

106] I heard a joke on the CBS Sunday Morning Show. I cannot remember who the comedian was, but it went something like this: A man was driving through town and was pulled over by the police for no apparent reason. When the police officer came to the window he asked the man, "Did you know your wife fell out of the car about one mile back?" The man responded, "Thank God!" The confused police officer responded, "What do you mean, 'thank God'?" The man responded, "I thought I was going deaf!" I shared this joke with my wife; she laughed.

107] Great day in Hibbing Cardinal Country! Amber Zapata, our point guard, was named MCAC North Division Player of the Week. Amber has had an outstanding freshman season and would have garnered a few more of these awards if we were having a better season. We are also picking up our second win of the season today, guaranteed! Fond Du Lac TCC is forfeiting the game. They are unable to complete their season again. I really don't know why we keep them in the league; they have had a program for five years and I don't think they have ever finished a season. We are now 2 & 24 on the season and have one more game, Mesabi at home on Saturday. No telling how that one will go, but like I said before, win or lose it is always fun when we play Mesabi in any sport.

2/21/2013

108] What is wrong with me? Last week my wife and I went to the Mary Wilson concert at the Reif Center in Grand Rapids, MN. We attend performances at the Reif Center about three or four times a year; it's almost always outstanding entertainment. This concert was also a good one. Ms. Wilson is one of the original Supremes. The performance started out with her singing a couple of Supreme songs. Mary's voice came across weak and raspy. Raspy I like, but the weak voice left me wondering if we had paid to watch an old icon try to recreate some fabulous songs. I started wondering just how old she is. I also caught myself noticing she had great legs and was actually in good shape for any age. She continued to sing and tell stories, and as her voice warmed up she really started knocking out every song. Besides the Supreme songs she did covers from Sting, Billy Joel, and the Rolling Stones. At one point she revealed to the audience that she had been performing for fifty-four years and was soon to turn sixty-nine.

Eventually, I got past the fact that I was listening to a sixty-nine-year-old woman sing "Baby Love," "Where Did Your Love Go," "Back in My Arms Again," and "Stop in the Name of Love," among others, and loved every minute of it. Ms. Wilson performed for over ninety minutes, nonstop, and took two curtain calls. To steal a line from a modern song, this girl was on fire!

Maybe there isn't anything wrong with me, and I'm just learning to appreciate someone aging and maintaining their inner and outer beauty. If I make it to sixty-nine, I can only hope to be able to instill this kind of joy in other people.

109] Whew! I am okay; the Sports Illustrated Swimsuit edition came in the mail this week, and I have enjoyed perusing through it. Apparently, Brent Musburger had it right, [See Random Thought #86], that ex-Miss Alabama [Katherine Webb] is one of the models.

3/2/2013

110] It is about 8:30 p.m. and I am sitting in a very comfortable chair in front of the fireplace at Spider Lake Lodge near Hayward, Wisconsin. Pam and I are on the second night of a two-night getaway. We have been back from dinner for a while and I have read through and glanced at every book and magazine that caught my attention. Pam seems to be deep into a book, so as often happens I am having some "Random Thoughts."

Last night we had a great dinner and I was able to partake in some of the latest brews at the Angry Minnow Brew Pub in Hayward. After dinner we went to a concert at the Park Theater; Kevin Bowe and the Okemah Prophets was the main band. Great concert and more beer from the Angry Minnow was available. The Park Theater is run by volunteers from a local radio station in Hayward. They do a great job; if you get a chance, attend a performance and support them.

This morning after breakfast, Pam and I went snowshoeing on the lake and went shopping in Hayward and had an early dinner at the Fireside. A sign in the men's bathroom at the Fireside caught my attention; it read: "If a man is alone in the woods and speaks and there is no wife to hear him, is he still wrong?"

Now it is a little after 9:00. As I said, I've read everything I care to read and I'm tired. Could be the snowshoeing, but throw in dinner and a couple of glasses of wine and put me in front of a fireplace, what would anyone expect? I'm sure love-making is out of the question; we did that last night and two nights in a row, who is kidding who here? Besides, Pam planned the getaway. It has been a great stay, and I think I'll just go to bed. I'm sure breakfast will be great in the morning, and who knows what exciting shopping stops Pam has planned for us on the drive home tomorrow.

3/14/2013

111] Interesting week: Saturday I was in Bradenton, Florida watching the Pirates play the Twins. Sunday I was assistant baseball coaching in New Port Richey, Fl; Hibbing CC vs. Pasco-Hernando CC. Monday we practiced in Tampa and then went to the beach in Clearwater, and it was 78 degrees. Tuesday our game was rained out. Wednesday we flew out of Orlando at 12:00 p.m.; it was 77 degrees. We arrived in Minneapolis, Minnesota at 5:30 and it was 28 degrees. I shoveled snow this morning in Hibbing, MN and went back to Minneapolis to recruit at the Minnesota State High School Girl's State Tournament.

112] I stopped in at Joe Senser's Bar and Grill tonight after the basketball games. I have a hard time believing I was just on the beach in Clearwater on Monday. Now I'm looking at women in sweaters and knit hats and listening to guys talking about golfing in a couple of months.

113] There are a couple of Green Bay Packers' fans sitting across the bar. These people wear Packer apparel year round. Pet peeve: if you are going to live here, at least back the teams here.

114] Just people watching; is a date going bad when the cell phones come out? Fat girl eating a salad and skinny girl eating wings and cheese curds; that just isn't fair!

115] What is up with all the ugly uniforms in the NCAA conference basketball tournaments?

116] Still people watching; drunk women in the bar are having serious, mature, conversations and are engaged. I don't think the men even hear each other.

117] Just heard a bad pick-up line: "I'm all about catch and release; I'm married."

118] I hear a lot of people talking about Netflix; is cable dead or just on the way out?

119] Two guys talking to a woman: ugly guy in pretty good shape, fat guy that is funny as hell. I'm pulling for the fat guy. Nope; ugly guy gets the girl.

120] I'm watching Oregon play Washington in the PAC 12 basketball quarter finals. Does Oregon pay for any of their uniforms, or are they just a Nike showcase?

121] I should stop taking notes on napkins; people are starting to stare.

122] In Minnesota you can't tell if people are leaving the bar or just going out to smoke. They still have to put on a coat, hat, and gloves. I wonder what the signal is to the servers?

123] Best sports comment I've heard tonight: "Matt Cassel is just an adult version of Christian Ponder."

124] If I do write a second book, maybe I should call it *My Version of Tweeting, hashtag: Random Thoughts.*

125] My bartender and server are married; I wonder if they split tips?

126] Does the mayhem guy on the Allstate Insurance commercials do all his own stunts? I love those commercials.

127] I'm listening to a couple of guys lamenting about their marriages. "I've got bills to pay; why would I spend money on a Valentine's dinner at the Olive Garden? I thought we could just do Papa Murphy's and stay at home. We haven't talked in a month!"
Second guy: "Is *Harry Potter* really done doing movies?
First guy: "Now we have to get a new fridge; where am I going to get that kind of money? My wife wants to go to marriage counseling. I think it would be a waste of time and money. I would rather just sit here with you drinking beer and talking it out."
Second guy: "My wife thinks I shouldn't be going out as much and spending money. Do you want to order another pitcher of beer and a pizza?"

128] I really need to stop writing on napkins; these people around me are getting paranoid.

129] Refer to Random Thoughts numbers 127, 119, and 117; same guys! I can't make this stuff up.

130] Unless I missed one or two, Joe Senser's has twenty big-screen televisions, all showing a different sporting event. Does this impress your date, or is that why Bruno Mars is playing in the background?

131] I'm sure I'm still sitting at a bar in Minneapolis, but I'm looking around and I see camouflage and Ducks Unlimited hats. I also see guy wearing a Duck Dynasty t-shirt and a Carhart coat, and he is talking to a preppy guy in a North Face coat. There is also a guy in a camouflage Georgia Bull Dog hat, mesh back. Are you kidding me? There are still more fat guys than black guys, so I'm sure I'm still in Minnesota.

132] Looking forward to tomorrow; I have to go to four games at the state tourney and take my son Blaine and his girlfriend Alex to dinner between sessions.

133] I have to get out of here and walk back to my hotel. What should I leave for a tip? I still don't know if my bartender and server are splitting tips, and more importantly, I might come-back Saturday night after the games.

3/16/2013

134] Couple of quick notes. I went to dinner with Blaine and Alex yesterday. I really hope those two stay together. I like her, and she seems to be doing a great job of training him. I don't know if he sees it yet, but he is being altered into marrying material.

135] Great 2A championship at the state tourney today. NREGH vs. Braham. Two of the top two players in the state, Rebekah Dahlman and Carlie Wagner, went head to head. Wagner broke her own scoring record with 50 points. Dahlman scored 32 points. NREGH won 60-59.

136] Stopped in at Senser's again tonight. I thought it would be fun to do a little St. Patrick's Day celebrating. I ended up being disappointed but on the other hand entertained. The place was packed. I thought it was for St. Patrick's Day, but it was also a pay-per-view UFC night. All twenty screens were showing UFC fights; no basketball or hockey.

I'm not into the UFC thing, so that is where the disappointment came from, but the people that showed up to watch it were very entertaining. Some very passionate fans! I'm not taking any notes on napkins tonight. I'd probably get beat up.

3/17/2013

137] Back in Hibbing. Happy St. Patrick's Day! I watched the weather report tonight; it was 25 degrees below zero earlier today. Last year we set an all-time record of 77 degrees. Why can't global warming just quit teasing us? The first day of spring is later this week, and we are supposed to have nighttime, below-zero temperatures in the 20s.

3/18/2013

138] First day of classes today, back from spring break; we were greeted with ten inches of snow this morning and 12-degrees-below-zero temperatures. Like my dad always said, "That is what keeps the riff-raff out." At the time he was right, but unfortunately he passed away before the meth heads started popping up. They don't seem to be curtailed by our weather.

3/20/2013

139] Today is the Spring Vernal Equinox; that is what I heard the weatherman call it this morning. Simply put, it is the first day of spring. This morning here in Hibbing, MN it was 3 degrees below zero, and we are expecting a high of 19 degrees. I don't know what the official measurement is, but we have a lot of snow. I do know that I am 6'2" tall and I noticed when I was shoveling yesterday that the snowbanks around my house are slightly above chest high.

I am predicting that the date the ice goes off the lakes and the date that baseball and softball fields are able to be played on around here are going to fall very close to each other. I am not an avid golfer, so I have no prediction about when people will get on the courses, and I am not all that concerned.

I am left to wonder, why do we live here? I also want a list of locations where global warming is actually taking place; maybe there is somewhere further south I can convince my wife to move to.

140] I just received an automated voicemail on my cell phone. "Congratulations; you have just won an all-expense paid cruise for two to the Bahamas!" I deleted it. Whoever these people are, they need to stop preying on innocent northern Minnesotans. The shipping lanes out of Duluth aren't even open yet!

3/21/2013

141] I teach a weight-training class at Hibbing CC. My students have to check in with me periodically with their workout logs. They have to record thirty weight-training days and fifteen third day or aerobic training days in the semester. The aerobic activities have to be a half-hour workout, minimum. One of my students stopped by my office yesterday to get their log sheet signed off on. When I checked the aerobic portion, they had eight days where they recorded "Sex" as their aerobic workout. I was torn between telling them it didn't count and telling them just how much I envied them. If I was keeping a log sheet, I know "Sex" wouldn't have made the list eight times in two months, and it definitely wouldn't be recorded as a half-hour workout. Eight times would be more like two years and thirty minutes total.

4/13/2013

142] Today is my son's 28th birthday. My wife and I called him this morning, woke him up, and sang him happy birthday. I hope this is not the highlight of his day.

143] I will be 54 years old on Monday. If I get there, I will have outlived my father. I've been thinking about this fact all year.

144] On Thursday I attended a funeral for a friend's 33-year-old daughter. This is a guy I have coached against for several years and have gotten to know pretty well. I wish I could say something or do something for him to help his pain go away. It was gut-wrenching to watch him carry a small wooden box containing the ashes of his daughter up to the altar.

Immediately after the funeral, I called my daughter and son to tell them how much I love them. I really wish we saw them more often, but that is not where life has us at this point in time.

I guess I am a little past my mid-life, and I haven't experienced a noticeable mid-life crisis to this point, other than the fact that I really want to retire in two years from my current job and move on to something else. How to accomplish this goal still is evading me.

There was a quote offered in the bulletin at the funeral. The quote was originally by Benjamin Franklin but was found in the writings of my friend's daughter. "Do not squander time… that is the stuff life is made of." I have been contemplating this quote for days now and trying to pin down the meaning in it for me.

145] Pam and I went to the Hibbing High School spring theater production last night. The play was Auntie Mame. Eighteen years ago, Pam and my son did that play at Central Lakes College in

Brainerd, Minnesota. Pam was Mame and Blaine played Young Patrick.

The Hibbing High School production was entertaining, but I'm not going to lie; I remember enjoying Auntie Mame a lot more when Pam and Blaine did it. I did enjoy watching Pam reminisce and surprise herself with how many of Mames' lines she remembered after eighteen years.

146] Shoveled snow again this morning; just a dusting last night. We have received about six inches since Thursday and are supposed to get 6-8 inches tomorrow and some more on Wednesday. I do miss coaching and playing baseball but not so much right now. I just hope the lakes are open for the fishing opener in May.

147] I've got to stop by the DMV and renew my drivers' license. My wife trimmed my eyebrows and had me clean up my own ear hair this morning. I'm sure my new license picture will be quite the glamour shot now. I just hope the DMV is open. I really don't want to have to get my eyebrows and ears trimmed again on Monday.

4/28/2013

149] It has been a while since I sat down to write any random thoughts. Not from lack of thinking, but mostly out of depression and not being able to wrap my head around some of the things that have been happening.

150] I did send Carrie Kozumplik and her husband a wedding present. Not necessarily true, but I'll say it anyway: better late than never.

151] On April 25, 2013 I celebrated my 54th birthday. I am particularly relieved to get by this one. As I said before, my father, Jack, died when he was 53. I really don't know what the significance of that is, but I am glad to have turned 54, and I am looking forward to whatever the next several years bring my way.

I received several well wishes, cards, and phone calls from family and friends. I also received three t-shirts. I am an avid collector of t-shirts. Jodi, one of our guests at the B&B, brought me a Louisville National Championship shirt; Go Cards! My mom sent me a Florida Gulf Coast University "Dunk City" shirt. She was in Fort Meyers, Florida during the NCAA play-offs.

My daughter, Lexie, sent a t-shirt that read "Ask Me about My Book" on the chest.

My wife surprised me with an orange cake. Orange cake and Carrot cake are my absolute favorites. I haven't had an orange birthday cake since I was a kid. Thanks to Pam and Duncan Hines, I was able to eat cake for breakfast all week.

152] This weekend, spring finally hit Hibbing, MN and most of our snow is gone. One week ago, April 19th, we received, hopefully, our last snowstorm. About 16 inches for those of us that count. The college closed down for the first time in three years. Normally this would have been very exciting, but I do not teach any classes on Fridays.

153] To say the least, it has been a long winter, and it is nice to think it might be over. Our baseball and softball teams played their first games outside in Minnesota this weekend. They now have two weeks left to complete their regular season games before play-offs start.

154] World events were devastating the last couple of weeks. Bombs in Boston, a factory blowing up in Texas, and a building collapse in Bangladesh. Hundreds were killed or injured. Hard to complain about a few extra weeks of winter when stuff like this is happening.

155] I have done a lot of weather watching the last few months; it's important as a groundskeeper at the Bed & Breakfast and a habit from several years of coaching baseball in Minnesota. Recently KBJR, the NBC television affiliate out of Duluth, MN, introduced the European model for reporting the weather. Much more difficult to decipher, but the accuracy is scary. Definitely takes away the guesswork.

156] My wife and I went to a movie on Friday night. We have reached the age where we, on occasion, go before 6:00 p.m. so we can get the discounted price and have popcorn for supper. Instead of dinner and a movie or movie and a dinner, we've got it down to a dinner/movie. Based on the number of people in attendance at these late afternoon matinees, we are not the only ones doing this.

The movie we attended was *The Big Wedding*. The movie starred Robert DeNiro, Susan Sarandon, Diane Keaton, Robin Williams, and Katherine Heigel. It also featured several other notable ac-tors and actresses.

I left the movie wondering about two of many unsolved mys-teries in my life. 1] Why do I continue to bother watching mov-ies that have a cast of several well-known stars? These types of movies are never any good. 2] Is there a rule of etiquette for de-ciding which armrests are yours when you have people sitting left and right of you?

157] Good night on the phones tonight; another volleyball recruit committed to attending Hibbing CC and playing this fall. Fi-nally; recruiting has been a little stagnant lately. I'm just about done with recruiting for volleyball, but things have to start picking up on the basketball side. A couple of weeks ago I got excited because two young ladies that I have been recruiting since September committed to attending Hibbing CC. My ex-citement was short-lived; they told me they just plan to play softball. I'm good friends with our softball coach, but this is still frustrating. Hopefully he can return the favor and find me a couple of basketball players.

2012 Hibbing CC Volleyball: [Photo by Mike Turnbull]
"I told them to ask for a Middle Hitter."
Front L-R: Brittany Gaskell & Courtney Wirtanen
Back L-R: Cassidy Baron, Jenna Massingill, Laurel Wright, Santa
Claus, Marina Carter, Ashley O'Hearon, and Emily Lange
[Photo by Mike Turnbull]

Audra McAllister 2012-2013 Hibbing CC Women's Basketball
[Photo by Jenny Konesky]
"It always warms my heart when a Cardinal runs over a Mesabi
Norsewoman!"

2012 Hibbing CC Volleyball [Photo by Brian Black]
#8 Marina Carter, #6 Jessie LaValley, #14 Emily Lange, Official
and ex-player; Nina [Lutmer] Kangas.
"We still didn't get any homer calls!"

Mike Turnbull [Photo by Mike Flaten]
"Ever stop to think…and never start again?"
[I can't be the only one!]

2013-2014 Hibbing CC Women's Basketball
[Photo by Don Monroe]
"Christina needs to pay attention."

Mike Turnbull

2012-2013 Hibbing CC Women's Basketball
[Photo by Larry Ryan Photography]
Front L-R: Tisha Rodgers & Courtney Wirtanen
2nd Row L-R: Amber Zapata, Arianna Zapata & Cassie
Hawkinson
3rd Row L-R: Leigh Lampton, Brittany Gaskell, Jasmin Freeman,
Audra McAllister & Allana Lampton

2012 Hibbing CC Volleyball
[Photo by Brian Black]
Top to Bottom: Marina Carter, Jessie LaValley & Courtney
Wirtanen
"You gotta love the enthusiasm!"

Mike Turnbull

2013-2014 Hibbing CC Women's Basketball
[Photo by Gary Giombetti]
L-R: Danni Bruns, Christina Wickingson, Courtney Wirtanen,
Taylor Martin and Ashlyn Norman
This was a very special season. These ladies get all my respect;
they played our last fourteen games with five players, no
substitutes. #FAB FIVE

2013-2014 Hibbing CC Basketball [Photo by Mike Flaten]
Mike Turnbull and the FAB FIVE

Mike Turnbull in another random t-shirt. [Photo by Mike Flaten]
"Like Spam, I've been around longer than you think, I am versatile and despite being underappreciated, go well with most anything."

Danni Bruns 2013-14 Hibbing CC Women's Basketball
[Photo by Don Monroe]
"Please, go in this time!"

2012 Hibbing CC Volleyball [Photo by Brian Black]
"All In!"

Mike Turnbull hanging out
in Bentleyville

[Photo by Emily Lange]

"I have always liked
Penguins!"

2013-2014 Hibbing CC Women's Basketball
[Photo by Don Monroe]
"Really, we can win this!"

2013 HIBBING CC VOLLEYBALL [Photo by Mike Turnbull]
Every volleyball season we stop at roadside landmarks and take team photos, this one is under the Big Catfish in Wahpeton, North Dakota.
L-R: Sami Cromley, Courtney Wirtanen, Gabby Sundquist, Cassidy Baron, Christina Wickingson, Laura Badavinac, Laurel Wright and Ellen Lescarbeau

2013 Hibbing CC Volleyball [Photo by Mike Turnbull]
Another HCC Volleyball tradition is going to the Potato Days
Festival in Barnesville, MN. We always enter four of our players
in the Mashed Potato Wrestling Tournament. This is our 2013
entrants getting pumped up for their tag team match.
L-R: Christina Wickingson, Sami Cromley, Gabby Sundquist and
Ellen Lescarbeau

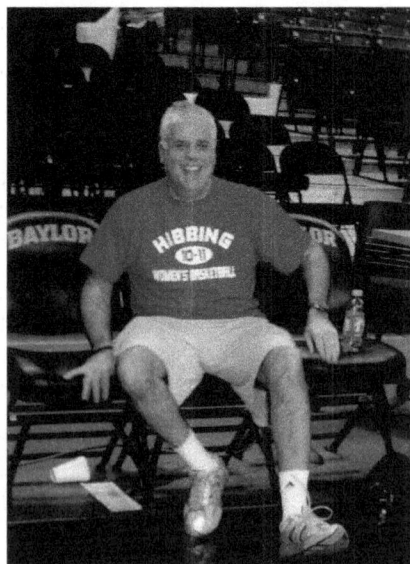

Mike Turnbull Waco, Texas
December 29, 2011

[Photo by Hunter Naisbitt, my
unofficial publicist]

"Living the dream!" [Until
security said we had to leave.]

"This is why I love Minnesota summers!"
[Photos by Mike & Pam Turnbull]

Finding the Walleyes.

Actually catching one!

Grilling it fresh.

Fresh Walleye, garlic
bread and a cold beer!

Winter of 2013-2014
The back of the Mitchell-Tappan House Bed and Breakfast.
"Worst winter ever!"

Winter 2013-2014;
Front of Mitchell-Tappan House Bed and Breakfast. I did find the front sidewalks sometime that day while shoveling.

This is the Antique Archaeology Van that Steve Rannikar and I chased after on I-80 in Iowa, just to find out it wasn't Mike and Frank from "American Pickers."

March 5, 2014 Sidewalk next to Mitchell-Tappan House Bed & Breakfast in Hibbing, MN
"This is why Pam & I are leaving for Florida today!"

March 13, 2014
Sidewalk by Kip & Carol Johnson's Town Home in Fort Meyers, FL.
"I envy the groundskeeper in this neighborhood!"

St. Petersburg Marina, St. Petersburg, FL Sunrise March 15, 2014. "How good is a cup of coffee, when you are looking at this? I can't believe I will be waking up in Hibbing, MN tomorrow morning."

Mike Turnbull

Rochester
COMMUNITY AND TECHNICAL
College *GET THERE*

OFFICE OF THE PRESIDENT

April 13, 2010

Kenneth Simberg, Provost
Hibbing Community College
1515 E. 25th Street
Hibbing, MN 55746

Dear Ken:

As you know, Rochester Community and Technical College's left-fielder Grant Ignatius suffered a heart attack during last Friday's baseball game with Hibbing. After administering CPR and four AED shock treatments, Grant was transported to St. Mary's Hospital where he remained in a medically induced coma until Sunday evening. On Monday, Grant was coherent, responding to commands, eating regular food and enjoying the company of teammates and well-wishers. He continues to improve, doctors are hopeful for a full recovery and Grant is hoping for release later this week.

I'm also writing to tell you how proud I was of the Hibbing coaching staff and team. Coach Mike Turnbull was supporting our coaching staff as they huddled near Grant. As our team gathered on the field to pray, what a moving sight it was to see the Hibbing players join them. That wonderful gesture of support was captured by the local NBC affiliate and has been replayed several times. Over the last few days a number of college staffers and community members have commented on that terrific show of sportsmanship. As the ambulance pulled away, Mike was right there telling Coach Hucke to gather with our players while he and the Hibbing team took to the field raking, pulling up the bases and gathering equipment.

Grant's incident is a good reminder on how fragile life is (even for a 19 year-old athlete), how we all too often take for granted the excellent health care services we enjoy, how many of life's lessons occur outside the classroom and how important it is to remember that there's much more to a game than winning. I'll keep you posted on Grant's progress. Please pass along my compliments and sincere thanks to your coaches and team...they are a class act!

Sincerely,

Don Supalla
President

CC   President Sue Collins
*   Mike Turnbull*

ROCHESTER COMMUNITY AND TECHNICAL COLLEGE

[See thought #72.]

64

HI & LOIS ©2012 by King Features Syndicate, Inc. World rights reserved.

(MORE)
RANDOM THOUGHTS

5/7/2013

158] This past weekend, Wisconsin held their 2013 Fishing Opener. I hope it went better in the rest of the state as opposed to northwest Wisconsin. The Governor's opener was scheduled for Cable, WI; they had twenty inches of ice and a foot of snow on some of the area lakes.

I did not participate in the Wisconsin opener, but I did watch the news reports on television. I'm sure it wasn't funny for the people that need to make money off the fishing industry, but I couldn't help but laugh when I saw a live broadcast in front of a bar in Cable and there were a dozen snowmobiles parked in the background. I don't know how many fish were caught, but I hope at least the bars and cafes did well.

159] The Minnesota Fishing Opener is this weekend. It has been a lot warmer this week, but it still is not looking very promising for northern Minnesota. I plan to skip the opener and take my wife and mother-in-law out for Mother's Day dinner. I hope to go fishing the weekend after the opener; my boat is not equipped for breaking ice.

160] Recruiting continues to move along. We signed another volleyball player today and hope to sign another. Recruiting on the basketball side of things needs to pick up — I've even started working on players from Poland, Croatia, and Denver, Colorado. We'll see how that goes.

5/29/2013

161] Last Wednesday, I decided to treat myself and go to Minneapolis, MN to watch the first day of the Big Ten Baseball Tournament. My wife thought I should take her car because she thought she had heard some odd noises coming from under my truck. Of course, I said everything would be fine and took my truck.

I made the 3 ½ hour drive to Minneapolis, and on the way down my dash gauges shutdown once and came back on eventually. I went to two games, ate dinner, and left. On the way out from Target Field, my truck died at the corner of Washington and Hennepin in downtown Minneapolis. I called for tow service. An hour and a half later, the tow truck showed up. Turns out my alternator was fried. The driver towed me to a garage, and they were able to replace the alternator, and by 11:00 p.m. I was on my way back to Hibbing. I arrived home about 2:30 a.m. To her credit, my wife did not greet me with an "I told you so!" She hit me with that later in the day when she saw the $600+ bill I left on her desk.

I love watching college baseball, but not at this price!

162] I'm on a roll. I may have mentioned before that this is my second book. The first was *Random Thoughts of a Stupid Man*. I was supposed to receive my first royalty check this past April. I received notice in early April that 2 Moon Press, my publisher, had been sold and was changing locations. They said they would be up and running after a short delay for the business transfer. I have lost all forms of contact with them in the past several weeks.

Yesterday, while searching the internet, I discovered an article from the Battle Creek Enquirer titled: "2 Moon Press: Abrupt Closure Sparks Probe." All I have been able to find out is that there is an ongoing investigation. At this point, I don't know if I'll ever see my royalties. My wife's response: "You sure know how to pick them."

163] My wife left me today. She just packed up, got in her new Cadillac, and left for the Twin Cities this morning. Luckily I remembered that she and my daughter are flying out to the east coast to celebrate my daughter's 30th birthday. Not to panic; I'm pretty sure she'll be back in a week.

She was smart enough not to leave me alone to run our Bed & Breakfast. I'll still be second in command, and Barb Anderson will run the show.

164] Am I the only person that does not think Ken Jeong is funny? I have seen him in commercials, *Hangover* movies, and the television show, *Community*. I just don't get his act; I find him to be more obnoxious than funny. Based on his popularity, I'm guessing I'm in the minority.

165] The school year has come to a close. That makes 32 years of teaching and coaching for me now. I have my goal set now to retire from teaching and coaching in 2 years.

166] I think I am having a mid-life crisis. I am planning on going to look at a lake cabin tomorrow. If I like it, I hope to find a way to convince Pam we should buy it when she gets back from her trip.

6/7/2013

167] It is June; according to most, one of the summer months; two days ago the temperature did not surpass 50 degrees.

168] My wife Pam returned from her vacation out east yesterday. She and my daughter Lexie had a great time. I can't tell you how glad I am that she is home. I asked to be fired from my

temporary inn-keeping job immediately. Hopefully I never get promoted above groundskeeping again.

Thank God Pam had the wisdom to bring in Barb, Connie, and Miranda to help while she was gone. If the Bed & Breakfast would have been left solely in my care, we would have been cancelling reservations. I don't know how Pam does all this on her own; it is mind boggling!

169] Pam does not like the cabin on Ely Lake, so the search continues, at least in my mind.

170] Once again, Pam is right; I do know how to pick them [# 162]. I have received a little more information on the investigation of the publisher of my first book.

The previous owner is saying the current owner is at fault for the closure, and the current owner is saying the previous owner is at fault. I really don't know what to think or how long this will take to sort out. I am always the optimist, so I am hoping it plays out well for me and the other authors involved.

171] I read the other day that the average American male spends seven years in the bathroom during their lifetime. I can't help but wonder: does that include standing in line at urinals in stadium bathrooms? I also wonder how much time would be knocked off if teenage boys just read the paper when sitting in the bathroom.

6/14/2013

172] I finished a volleyball camp in Pine River, MN last night and then drove to Minneapolis to meet my son Blaine at the Twins vs. Phillies game, his treat, my belated birthday gift. After the game I stayed at my mom's and had a very good visit. It was great to spend time with them, and I was happy that my mom seems to be doing well.

173] I left my mom's this morning at 6:00 a.m. to drive to Omaha, Nebraska for the College World Series. Still hit rush-hour traffic, another reminder about why I don't want to live in a big city.

I have said this before, but the College World Series has become my absolute favorite sporting event to attend. The baseball is outstanding, the atmosphere is great, and I seem to meet new people every year, along with several others I have come to know over the years. The city of Omaha does a fantastic job of hosting the series, and it should never leave there.

My daughter and son-in-law live in Auburn, NE, about an hour south of Omaha, so I get to stay with them and drive in and out of Omaha.

174] I'm staying at the Western Inn in Council Bluffs, IA for one night. I'll go to the first games tomorrow and then drive down to Lexie and Jeff's tomorrow night. I think I'll walk over to the Spillway Bar for dinner and a couple of beers.

175] I'm done with dinner, and beers are 2 for 1, so I think I'll stay here for a while and take some napkin notes.

There are about twenty people in the bar. A couple across the bar is doing a little complaining about the music on the juke box. Some of us have told the husband to part with some of his money and pick a few of his own songs. The guy finally caves in and selects two songs: "Moon Light Serenade" and "In the Mood." Great music, but when is the last time you ever heard big band music playing in a Sports/Country bar?

The man comes back to the bar and asks his wife to dance. They spin around the floor for both songs; great stuff! After dancing, he sits down and starts entertaining us with WWll stories, and his wife tells about the end of the war and going to pick up her husband in New York, when he got back from Europe.

I don't spend a lot of time in bars, but I'm glad I didn't miss this opportunity. Time to go back to my room and go to bed. I'm excited about opening day. I'm looking forward to seeing Mississippi State and Indiana. It has been a while since the Bulldogs have been here and Indiana has never played in the series. LSU is back in the series, so I know their fans will show up in mass numbers; they love their Tigers.

176] When I got back to the hotel, I met an elderly gentleman sitting on a bench in front of the hotel. He asked me where I was from and if I had time to visit for a while. Turns out he is from Mississippi and was in town for the College World Series; he has been attending since 1972.

Most of our conversation was about baseball and how cold it can get in Minnesota. The one thing he said, though, that I won't forget, pertained to air conditioners. He blamed air conditioners for being the downfall of neighborhoods. He said everyone used to sit out on their porches in the evenings and people would walk around the neighborhood and visit with each other. When people started putting in air conditioners that all stopped. People closed their doors and windows and cranked up the air conditioners to cool off. Nobody came out and visited anymore. I wonder what his take is on cell phones and Facebook.

6/17/2013

177] I have been at the CWS for two days now. I have seen three of the four games. I missed the second game yesterday. I couldn't get back into general admission and reserved was all sold out. I'm blaming the LSU fans for that. I think I will start buying reserved seats next year. It is getting impossible to get general admission for game two if you are in the park for game one. People start lining up two to three hours in advance.

I did get to go out for a Fathers' Day dinner with Lexie and Jeff last night, so things do work themselves out.

178] I got to both games today, but I had to do some wheeling and dealing with a ticket scalper for a reserved seat for game two. I'm real proud; I got a $35 dollar ticket for $35 and two general admission tickets. Great seat: row 8, right by third base.

179] I was listening to ESPN radio on the drive back to Lexie and Jeff's tonight. They were talking about motivational speakers, videos, and CDs. It sounded more like a commercial than a discussion until a listener called in with what I thought was a very astute comment. The caller said if you decide to spend a couple hundred dollars to see a motivational speaker or buy a video or CD series, don't do it; you are already a motivated person.

6/18/2013

180] Last day in Omaha. I'll watch an elimination game at 2:00 and then make the ten-hour drive back to Hibbing. Should be fine; I love driving at night. I also have to find a shirt for Steve Ranikar. He couldn't make the trip this year. I also have to find Chris Vito a hat. Chris has never made the trip to Omaha, but he puts a hat request in every year. An odd tradition, but I enjoy the hunt.

181] When I came out of the stadium I had several missed calls on my phone, from my wife, daughter, and sisters; that can't be a good thing. Turns out, my mom fell in her condominium and was not discovered for two days. They have taken her to the hospital by ambulance. A nurse told my sister to start calling in her family.

I will pick up my sister Terri in Austin, MN and hopefully we can make it to Minneapolis by midnight or so. I can only pray my mom hangs on until we get there.

182] It is about 8:00 p.m. My sister Lisa just called and she said my mom says she is dying. The doctor says my mom isn't showing the signs of a dying person, but she is talking like one. They are transferring her to another hospital and putting her in Intensive care.

The EMTs asked my sister about my dad. She told them that my dad died in 1989. They thought that was odd because my mom has said she saw my dad and talked to him.

6/19/2013

183] Long night; spent several hours watching over my mom in the ICU. They have her stabilized and it seems like she'll be pulling out of it. The nurse sent us all home to get a couple hours of sleep.

184] 10:00 a.m. and we are all back in my mom's room. She seems to have turned the corner. We asked her about talking to my dad. She was very detailed in relaying that experience to us. She said he wasn't there anymore, though that he had told her she can't go with him yet and that her kids and grandchildren still needed her. She said that she argued with my dad but to no avail; she couldn't go with him.

This all makes perfect sense to me. My mom is a tough, strong-willed person. I have a feeling God didn't want to argue with my mom so he sent my dad to comfort her and set her straight.

185] My mom is going to be okay. They will transfer her to a regular room tomorrow. I'm going home for a few days and I'll come back down to Minneapolis later. Hibbing is about four hours away.

6/22/2013

186] My sister Lisa and her husband Mark took my mom out of the hospital today. They brought her to a nursing home in Austin, MN so she can do her rehabilitation until she gets her strength back. We will find out what comes next after that. The doctors and occupational and physical therapists will tell us if she can go back home on her own or needs to go to an assisted living facility. This is not a discussion or decision that any of us are looking forward to.

I'm glad that they were able to get her a room at the nursing home in Austin, because my sister Terri works there and can see my mom every day.

6/26/2013

187] I'm going to go to Austin tomorrow and spend a couple of days with my mom and sister Terri. My sisters Lisa and Stacie went down and spent the day yesterday and Terri has been there every day.

I will assume my role as the "Golden Child." Lisa and Stacie and their families live near my mom and Terri calls her every day at home. They do a lot more for my mom than I ever do. I call once every couple of weeks and see my mom maybe four times in a good year. When I do call or go to see my mom, her world stops and it is all about her Michael. I know this irritates my sisters to no end, but hey, I am the oldest and I am the only boy!

188] Might have dodged a bullet yesterday. Pam has wanted to expand her Bed & Breakfast business and open a second house. We put an offer in on a house last Friday; the owners have decided they are not ready to sell. Maybe I can get her to start entertaining the idea of a cabin again.

6/27/2013

189] On my way to Austin, MN, my sister Terri called and said my mom has been moved to the Emergency Room; she got dizzy and collapsed during a physical therapy session. I got to Austin about 2:00 p.m., my mom looked terrible, about as old as I've ever seen her look. She is really having a rough time.

The doctor released my mom at about 6:30 p.m. and let my sister and I take her back to her room at the rehabilitation center. I stayed with her until about 10:30; she seems to be doing a lot better. Quite the roller coaster the last couple of weeks. My mom did say she wants me to check out assisted living places in Austin.

6/28/2013

190] I checked out an assisted living facility in Austin this morning for my mom. Very nice place, and the room has a view of the river; my mom loves being by water. I talked to one of the residents in the hall. She asked me if I was planning on moving in soon and said they could use more males. Am I really looking that old?

Later I went to the rehab center to visit my mom. She is doing a lot better but has a long way to go. I showed her the information on the assisted living facility, and she was very receptive. I went to my sister's house in the afternoon and did some yard work for her.
In the evening I went back to visit my mom and had dinner with her. I thought the dinner was fine, but she has been complaining about the food. Solved that one; my mom is a diabetic and has high blood pressure, so they have eliminated salt and sugar from her foods. She is eating the way she should and not the way she eats at home.

We watched the Twins on television and discussed a lot of things. We talked about her grandchildren, my son planning on moving in with his girlfriend, how she first met my dad, and eventually her health and the future. She did inform me that she does not want to stay in Austin. She either wants to go back to her condominium or an assisted living facility in the Minneapolis area. We'll just have to wait and see what the doctor says when her rehabilitation is over.

6/29/2013

191] I am going home today. I saw my mom this morning and walked her over to a Bingo game; she was ready to relax and win some money. I'm glad I got to spend time with her and my sister. I don't see either one of them nearly enough.

192] Found the Twins game on an AM radio station. I love listening to baseball on AM radio. There is just something about it that takes me back to summer nights in my childhood. If I have a game to listen to, I can drive forever.

193] I hate traffic. I am stuck on I-35 just south of Minneapolis. It is bumper to bumper and there is an accident up ahead. How do these people put up with this every day? Rolled down the windows—big mistake. A big turkey truck just pulled up alongside of me. Back to the air conditioner.

192] Is it true that the guy who wrote *Men are from Mars, Women are from Venus* is now divorced? If it is, I'm really disappointed. That kind of shoots a big hole in that guide to marriage. Throw that together with Dr. Spock's parenting guide and my professor in college that taught Courtship and Marriage ending his marriage by shooting his wife, and I'm left with only my parents' advice, my wife's guidance, and my own experiences to get me through the rest of my life. I hope God steps in every once in a while.

7/2/2013

193] I did some checking. Dr. John Gray, the author of *Men are from Mars, Women are from Venus*, was divorced but remarried. I don't really know if this adds to his expertise or not. I really have never figured out the logic of people who do marriage do-overs. I love my wife and I cherish being married to her, but I can't see going through the whole process with someone else again. I know I have to have another colonoscopy, but that is a necessity of good health. I know what you are thinking, "Did he just compare marriage to a colonoscopy?"

194] My wife Pam has basically squashed the idea of getting a cabin for now, so I renewed the search for a new boat. Wish me luck!

7/3/2013

194] This whole having your parents get old thing really sucks! Today it is my father-in-law's turn. He is having a tumor removed from his bladder today. My wife and her family went to Duluth today to take him for his surgery. It is supposed to be an outpatient procedure; I pray all goes well.

195] Just got word today that one of my basketball players can't afford to return to college this fall for her sophomore year. Hopefully the next news I hear is a yes from one of the players we are still recruiting.

I get to see every day how hard it is for kids to pay for college. I wish our Congressional members and state legislators would spend some time with these kids before the vote again to raise tuitions or the interest rates on student loans. Pretty soon, if not already, the middle class is going to be priced out of college.

196] I'm looking forward to going to Vito's cabin tonight to watch the Eveleth fireworks and going to Ely for the weekend to spend some time up there.

I love watching fireworks— always have! This is a banner summer; we had fireworks at the Hibbing Raceway last weekend, tonight in Eveleth, and in Ely on the 4th! Once again, I'm living the dream!

7/8/2013

197] I'm driving to Austin, MN today to see my mom. Hopefully she will be done with her rehab at the nursing home and I can take her back to her own place on Wednesday. I'm not totally convinced she can go home and take care of herself. My sisters are convinced we should let her try before we start seriously consider assisted living.

I am driving alone with just my own thoughts, so I'll jot a few down and try to record them later.

198] Pam and I were in Ely for the 4th. There were a ton of people in town. Sheridan Street was packed for the parade, the weather was great, and we were able to see a lot of people in Whiteside Park after the parade. We went to Scotty Magie's home on Burnside Lake later in the afternoon and came back into town and watched a terrific fireworks display from the front of Grand Ely Lodge. Big traffic jam after the show; it took us about a half hour to make the two mile drive back to my in-laws' house. Ely is just crazy on the 4th!

199] Pam had her 35th High School Class reunion on Friday and Saturday, the class of 1978. Pam had a great time and so did I. It is still fun to be a spouse when you know most of the class; advantage of graduating from a small school.

Several of the guys I talked to were already retired or thinking hard about it. I was envious. I am working on it, shooting for two years. Most everyone had the same idea, retire and go off the grid or at least find something to do where you could just work when you felt like it. I get this; just get to a place in your life where maybe your life is your life. Grand concept, but I'm pretty sure it still requires a sufficient income and health insurance.

The women that got involved in these retirement discussions didn't seem to get the off-the-grid concept. Most of them seemed to think going without the daily demands of work and family would be boring.

200] On Saturday night her class had dinner and a social at the Long Branch on Fall Lake in Winton, MN, just outside of Ely. Around 9:30 p.m. it was hot and muggy, and the mosquitoes started to swarm the place. Kind of broke up an otherwise great party. A lot of us moved the party to town and an air conditioned Antler Lounge at the Grand Ely Lodge.

Until the party broke up, I don't know what was more entertaining: watching people try to swat mosquitoes and carry on conversations or watching Pam and many of her female classmates deal with the heat. I'm pretty sure most of the women there were either pre, post, or currently menopausal. They all seemed to be having one big communal hot flash.

201] It was really good to see Pam get out for a couple of nights and loosen up and have a good time. She works extremely hard running our very successful Bed & Breakfast in Hibbing, and it is basically a 24/7 operation. The time she gets away is well deserved, and I wish she could have more time like that.

7/11/2013

202] I drove back from my mom's in Minneapolis last night. I was able to get her out of the nursing home in Austin and bring her home. I also managed to get my sister Terri's backyard fence painted. She now has a white picket fence and she is thrilled. It is not often I get to help her out; it felt good.

203] I left Minneapolis at 7:00 p.m. to miss rush hour. That was the plan anyway. The normal drive from I-94 across 694 East to I-35 North is usually about 15 minutes, but because of construction and at least one accident it took a little over two hours.

A few things came to mind while sitting stuck in traffic. First of all why couldn't I get cell phone service? I never have a problem in the Twin Cities. Secondly, I have spent way too much time stuck in traffic this summer and I hate traffic. I'll never complain about the occasional delay at a 4-way stop in Hibbing again. I also couldn't help but question my theory of staying in the left lane when traffic is backed up. I knew that the right lane was closed ahead; there were several warning signs. The right lane flowed better the entire time, despite all the mergers. I was hardcore and didn't let anyone cut in. I refuse to give in to people who are cheating the system and drive in the closed lane for as long as they can or until the construction cones force them to merge.

If you are in the left lane and traffic is merging from the right, don't you have the right of way? Some people seem to think that merging is a right; I believe that it is a privilege!

We have on/off ramps in Minnesota on major highways, areas where traffic exits and enters within a couple hundred feet of each other. Not a bad system when traffic is light, but when traffic is heavy it is a nightmare. You might as well set up a figure eight track and call it a demolition derby race!

While stuck in traffic, I heard a commercial on the radio for a K-12 online school. The commercial had kids giving testimonials and saying things like: "It lets me work at my own pace." "I can spend more time with math and less time on history." "I don't have to carry books." "I can do it at home on my own schedule." "My mom doesn't have to drive me to school or pick me up."

It really scares me that kids could complete a K-12 education without ever setting foot in a school building. I would like to start an anti-online school commercial. I would say things like, If you don't want to develop social skills, go online. If you don't want to know your classmates, go online. If you don't want to learn anything about conflict resolution, go online. If you don't want to take physical education, music, or any art programs, go online. If you don't ever want to have a crush on a teacher, go online. If you have no desire to meet your high school sweetheart, go online. If you don't want to participate in sports, drama, band, student senate, or pep squad, go online. If you never want to worry about whether your picture is in the school yearbook, go online. If you don't want to shop for new school clothes and supplies every year, go online. [Okay, I'll admit, that might actually be a promotion for online schools.] If you never want to have to attend a class reunion, go online.

Basically what I am saying is if you want to lead your life living and learning from a desk chair or bed at home and not getting out into the real world, go online!

204] The first thing I had to do when I got my mom back to Minneapolis today was take her to buy a walker. The store had all kinds. She didn't want the two-button fold up with the tennis balls on the front, she went high end. Hot pink, some bling, wheels in the front and back, handbrakes, and a fold down seat. She should be all the rave when she goes to get her mail in the lobby.

I wasn't thinking; I should have talked her into the blue one so I would have a cool walker when the time comes. I guess I will just have to be the grumpy old guy with the hot pink walker when my day comes.

205] I am going to stop writing now and go home. I need to work on getting my new boat ready for the weekend. While we were in Ely over the 4th I bought a used fishing boat. It is a 1979, 16-foot Lund, side steer with a 50-horsepower, Mercury motor. Nice boat, mint condition; bought it from an elderly couple on White Iron Lake and it was only $2,400.

Truth be told, my father-in-law Rod paid for it and would not let me write the check. I attempted to argue, but he would not hear any of it. I was already indebted to him for who knows how much and now this. He is a stubborn guy and we never talk about it, but I love him dearly and he can call me "TURN-BULL" all he wants. [See Random Thought Number 22 in my first book, *Random Thoughts of a Stupid Man*.]

7/28/2013

206] Pretty busy last week. I directed a Volleyball camp in Springfield, MN. I have never been there before. Real nice town, well cared for school, and good kids to work with.

Springfield is a town of a little less than 3,000 people west of New Ulm and Sleepy Eye, MN on highway 14. At lunchtime I spent a little time driving around town looking at all the nice, old houses in town. That went well until a local police officer started following me around. The last three days I picked up something to eat and went and sat around at the park, read the newspaper, and ate lunch. He never stopped to talk to me, but that same police officer managed to cruise by at least once each day and check me out. I don't know if he was bored or somebody reported a creepy, old guy hanging out at the park. Either way, the citizens of Springfield should know they are being looked after.

207] On July 25th it was reported that over 500,000 Marijuana plants at a street value of over four million dollars had been found by law enforcement agents outside of Hinckley, MN. This is not earth-shattering news in east central Minnesota, but the quantity was impressive.

I am not a pot smoker but it was disturbing to read that the marijuana plants were going to be incinerated within the next couple of days. Was this announcement made so that federal agents could protect their newfound stash or to keep prospective thieves out of the evidence warehouse?

When I was a teenager and later in college, I'm pretty sure any time one of our beer parties was busted and the beer was confiscated, that beer found its way to some police officer's home. I'm not saying that the agents that made this Marijuana bust should keep the Marijuana, but maybe the State of Minnesota could have sold it to a state in which Marijuana is legal, or better yet maybe the city of Detroit, MI. It seems to me they need all the help they can get.

208] It was announced today that Anthony Weiner's [Carlos Danger] mayoral campaign manager is leaving him. Maybe Mr. Weiner's wife should follow his lead and Mr. Weiner should realize that New Yorkers are probably not interested in electing a sexting addict.

209] Yesterday my wife told me if I wanted to go see the Tall Ships in Duluth, MN to go ahead; she did not care to go. I was pretty sure this wasn't a set-up, so I went. I got to see about six of the ships and had lunch at the Canal Park Brew Pub. Despite bad weather, I had a great time.

The Tall Ships made their last appearance in Duluth in 2010. There weren't nearly as many people in attendance then. This year they estimated the three-day crowd total to be over 250,000. I had no problem parking but did not have a ticket to see the ships. I was still able to get close enough to see what I wanted to see; I just couldn't board the ships.

I've said this before, but if you ever get to see a Tall Ship Festival, whether it be in Duluth or some other port, seize the opportunity; you won't be disappointed.

210] Today Pam and I went to Ely, MN for the Blueberry Arts Festival. It gets bigger every year — another event to put on your bucket list. It is held the last week of July every year.

211] My mom is still back at her home, and her health seems to be improving and she is regaining her strength. She is definitely not out of the woods yet but definitely seems to be getting better. Hopefully the move to assisted living can wait for a while.

Pam's dad on the other hand is not doing so well. We saw him today and he is in a pretty weak state and having complications from his surgery. It is really starting to weigh heavy on Pam and her mother.

This whole cycle of life thing has consumed both Pam and I this summer. I know we aren't the first people to deal with aging parents and all that goes with it, but that doesn't make it any easier. I would love to say something insightful here, but I've got nothing!

8/7/2013

212] I am in Osseo, WI this week directing a Pacesetter Volleyball Camp at Osseo-Fairchild High School. Nice bunch of girls to work with in each session. I'm pretty sure this will be my last Pacesetter Camp. I have been directing Pacesetter Camps every summer since 1985. The most I did in any given summer was fourteen.

Working for Jeff McCarron, the owner of Pacesetter Camps, has been a pleasure and a very interesting ride. Jeff's concept was to bring camps to the high schools and make them affordable for the kids. Pacesetter offers Basketball and Volleyball camps and lets the individual schools set the times and age groups. Pacesetter provides the coaches. Pacesetter has also expanded and added basketball tournaments over the years. Regional and state tournaments are held all over Minnesota throughout the spring and summer.

I have had the opportunity to direct camps in Minnesota, Wisconsin, Iowa, and South and North Dakota. The camps have been held mostly in small, rural towns with an occasional Minneapolis, Saint Paul, Saint Cloud, or Sioux Falls thrown in there. I have been blessed to meet a lot of kids, coaches, parents, and local residents in those towns that I would otherwise have never have had the opportunity to meet.

The Pacesetter Coaches fraternity is a tight-knit group; I have always enjoyed the coaches I have had the opportunity to work with; great bunch of guys!

213] Osseo has been a treat; interesting town. I have bypassed Osseo many times but never stopped here. It is a small town about fifteen miles east of Eau Claire, just off of I-94. The thing that has caught my attention is the business creativity. There are several businesses that have multiple fronts under one roof. Yesterday, I stopped in the liquor store to pick up some beer. Turns out the liquor store is also a cheese shop, an antique store, and an espresso café, all under one roof. Tonight I went to a restaurant across the highway from my motel. The restaurant, a bar & grill, was attached to a hotel. I have seen that before, but also in the same building there was a beauty salon, an insurance office, and a hearing clinic.

This creative combination of businesses not only caught my attention, it seemed to be a very efficient way to do business in a small town and a great utilization of space. The true kicker in the deal was right behind the motel I am staying in. I want it to be known I did not shop there this week, but it still intrigued me. The store was an adult XXX store; the billboard advertising it is huge and faces east and west alongside I-94. I first noticed it last night when it was lit up. This morning I noticed they also have sheds and fish houses for sale on the lawn out in front of the store. How great would that be to tell your wife you are going to the adult XXX bookstore to look at sheds?

214] I watched the news tonight and then flipped to Sports Center. The news was dominated by Anthony Weiner and his campaign in New York; Sports Center couldn't seem to get away from Alex Rodriguez reports. When are these two going to realize their teams don't want them, their chosen profession doesn't want them, the media has tired of them, and they probably don't have a lot of support in or out of New York?

8/10/2013

215] Tomorrow night is our first night of volleyball practice for the 2013 season. I coach Women's Volleyball at Hibbing Community College in Hibbing, MN. It is always an exciting time of the year for me; I love the anticipation of a new season and the potential each season opens with.

On Friday a potential player came to my office to tell me she had decided to stay home and attend Hibbing CC. She went on to tell me how passionate she is about playing volleyball and couldn't see herself not playing. I thought we have eleven players so why not add another? I gave her the paperwork and told her to be in the gym Sunday night.

So I am expecting twelve players at our first practice, and I like what I'm looking at on paper.

8/11/2013

214] We had our team meeting and first practice tonight. Remember, I thought we were coming in with twelve players. Eleven showed up for the meeting; another player that was supposed to pick the twelfth up said she received a text from that player saying she had decided not to play for financial reasons. After the team meeting, the players went to the locker room to get dressed for practice. One player had somewhat of a panic attack after the meeting and decided she couldn't do this; she'd had no idea we had such a busy schedule. These kids have had our daily schedule in their hands since late May!

Anyway, we'll be back in practice for day two tomorrow night. The first practice went well with the ten players we did have, and we can work with that.

215] Second day of volleyball practice; we are practicing tonight at 6:00 p.m. Two more players just left my office. They turned in their equipment and said they will not be able to play. One said there's too much conflict with work. Again, they have had our schedule since May! The second girl, the one that gave me the passionate speech three days ago, said she has lost the burn and desire to play volleyball and thinks she should step away while it is early in the season so she doesn't let anyone down. Too late!

When we come in for practice tonight, I hope there are no more surprises. We are at eight, and we'll have to make it work! I like the eight we have and there is no need to cut anybody from the team. They should all be happy; they are all going to play and will all have a significant role on the team. I just hope we can stay healthy.

I am glad I can write this stuff down. It wouldn't be fair to bring any of this frustration home and dump it on my wife.

10/19/2013

216] I had a northern Minnesota experience today that I have never had before. I started to try to rake and mulch my yard one last time late this morning. I finished the raking, but before I could finish mulching the leaves and cutting the grass it started snowing pretty hard. Cutting path through the snow across the yard was a unique sight to behold. I know my wife and some of our guests at our B&B got a kick out of it.

217] I attended a personal pre-retirement seminar in St. Paul the other day. I really think I can pull off retirement after the 2014-15 school year. I still have a lot of checking to do on health insurance costs, though. I think President Obama better do some checking on his plan, also; there seem to be some possible serious glitches.

12/22/2013

218] Pam and I went to the Donny & Marie Osmond Christmas Concert at the Target Center in Minneapolis last night. Not at the top of my bucket list, but definitely a big one for Pam. I will admit, though, they put on a great show and it was worth every dime to see how excited Pam was to see Donny perform live after all these years of unbridled infatuation. She wasn't the only 50+ year old woman in the crowd that was just a little excited.

12/26/2013

219] Another great Christmas in Ely, MN. Pam and I, Lexie and Jeff, and Blaine and his girlfriend Alex all went to Ely and spent Christmas Eve and Day with the Loes and some of the LaTourells. Nothing completes Christmas more for me than sitting in the church, surrounded by family and friends, while the church is only lit by the candles being held by the people and everyone sings Silent Night backed by the church bells ringing. It is one time every year that the world seems right to me and at peace.

220] I dropped a small hint this year that I would like the Hallmark Christmas ornament that depicts Clark Griswold, from the movie *Christmas Vacation*, plugging in the light cords. I guess my wish was heard; I received that ornament plus the one with the tree on top of the car. I also received a glass Moose Head mug and a wine bottle stop in the same Moose Head design.

This all goes well with the Chicago Blackhawks Griswold hockey jersey I received from my children a few years ago. Not to be greedy, but if anyone reads this, the white sweater and black dickey that cousin Eddie wore in the movie are at the top of my list for next year.

As you can guess, I love that movie and I hope they never try to remake it. I saw *Christmas Story 2* this year and it was terrible.

12/28/2013

221] Pam and I went to Melissa [Weez] Nyberg and Matt Erickson's wedding last night. Beautiful wedding and a great time was had by all at the reception. There were five kids in the wedding that I have coached in one sport or another over the years and several other ex-players at the wedding. I can't begin to tell you how enjoyable it was to just visit with them and hash over some very fond memories.

12/30/2013

222] Tomorrow is New Year's Eve and it only seems right to reflect on 2013. Overall, it was a good year. My volleyball team did stay healthy and finished a couple games out of the top four. The 2013-14 Basketball season has been a challenge; we have played 13 games with pretty much six players. We were expecting to have eight after the Christmas break, but one of our players blew her ACL and will need surgery and one player we were waiting for grade eligibility on might not be eligible. Right now that puts us at five healthy, eligible players. We come back to practice on January 2nd and I am hoping we can pick-up a couple more players before the conference season starts. Coaching at a Division lll Junior College has always been interesting, but it seems to be getting harder and harder to find local kids that want to make the commitment to the rigors of being a student-athlete in a non-scholarship setting. The young ladies I have playing this year are a great bunch of people and fairly talented, but we need some depth.

223] During the week of Christmas, I was able to watch the Today Show on NBC every day. Savannah, Natalie, Willie, and Dillon did a great job while Matt and Al were on vacation. It is the first time I really enjoyed the show since Ann Curry left. Maybe they should let Matt and Al have more time off.

224] I'm still trying to decide if I should be alarmed by the credit card scandal at Target. I did make a purchase at Target on the last Sunday that something may have happened to, but it seems to be okay.

225] Today I started the annual cleaning of my office. I came across a book of questions by Tim O'Brien; #19: "Wouldn't it be fun to take the lights at a sports arena and hook them up to the clapper?"

226] The Minnesota Vikings played their last game at the Hubert H. Humphrey Metrodome yesterday. They have played there since 1982, and now the stadium is considered obsolete. They will move into a new stadium in two years. They will play at TCF Bank Stadium, the home of the Minnesota Gophers, for the next two seasons. It will be like old times; Minnesota fans can see two bad football teams share the same venue again. The Gophers are getting better, but the Vikings were pretty disappointing this year.

I wasn't able to be at the Dome for yesterday's game, but my son and I did go to the Eagles game two weeks ago. It was sad when we walked out for the last time and got blown through the doors. I'll miss that rush of air as you exit the Dome. Anyone who ever attended a game in the Metrodome knows what I'm talking about.

227] Another question from Tim O'Brien's Book of Questions, #140: "How many people thought of the Post-It Note before it was invented but just didn't have anything to jot it down on?"

228] Great news today; I may have found a new publisher for my first book, *Random Thoughts of a Stupid Man*. We'll see how that goes. If it works out, maybe I'll be able to get another collection of *Random Thoughts* published. [Flash to the future:] If you are reading this right now, I did find a new publisher and you are reading my second book, *Did I Say That Out Loud? [More Random Thoughts of a Stupid Man]*.

229] This might be a good place to end this collection of thoughts. That said; just a few parting thoughts. 1] Blaine, marry Alex; she is good for you and we'd love to have her in the family. 2] Lexie, hopefully this is the year that you and Jeff have your first child. We all know you have been trying, and your mom and I would love to be grandparents, and you and Jeff will be great parents. No pressure! 3] Pam, I really hope I can find a way to at least semi-retire at the end of the 2014-15 school year. I promise I will find ways to stay out of your way. 4] Mom, Rod, Bill, and Joan, stay healthy; we all still need you in our lives.

1/1/2014

230] This quote was sent to me today and I had to share it! "Today is the first blank page of a 365 page book. Write a good one." - Brad Paisely

1/2/2014

231] I sent the previous quote out to some people with New Year's greetings. Kasey Palmer, one of my ex-players, responded with this one: "What the New Year brings to you will depend a great deal upon what you bring to the New Year" - Vern McClellan

1/3/2014

232] I was going to quit writing at number 229, but my basketball team is trying to something special and I think it is worth following. I know I am intrigued.

We have five players and 14 games left to play in the regular season. We play two non-conference games this weekend and start conference play on Wednesday.

233] Back at the hotel, just called the game into the newspaper. We lost by 30+ to one of the top teams in the state.

All five players went 40 minutes, nobody fouled out, and nobody got hurt. We live for another day! We play Riverland CC tomorrow.

1/4/2014

234] I would say unbelievable, but I saw it and I believe it. We beat Riverland 57-56 in overtime. Played the last two minutes with 4 players; Courtney Wirtanen fouled out. You have no idea how proud I am of these young ladies—they're a tough bunch of kids!

1/8/2014

235] We played our first conference basketball game at home against Rainy River tonight. We won 64-54. We might be on to something—only 12 turnovers and nobody fouled out. Pretty good formula for any basketball team's success, but especially when you only have five players.

236] When did it become acceptable for the receiver to not respond to e-mails and phone messages and assume the sender would understand the sender knows this means their response is no? I have sent several e-mails and phone messages to seven students on campus that could help our basketball team with our lack of numbers. Only one of them has responded and let me know that they could not play. I have not heard anything from the other six.

In my mind I am left to wonder: did they get the messages or are they just mulling it over? Or are they just ignoring me until I just stop bugging them? The lack of personal communication drives me crazy.

1/10/2014

237] Basketball practice went well yesterday and today. We still have just our five players and they are feeling pretty good about Wednesday night's win. I'm not worried about them getting over-confident because having only five players tends to keep a team humble.

We play our rival tomorrow at home, Mesabi Range. They have a good team made up of eleven players. I know it is 5 on 11, but I like our chances.

1/11/2014

238] Tough loss today! We lost 68-66 in overtime to Mesabi. Nobody fouled out, everyone went 45 minutes, but we had 33 turnovers. We are all disappointed with the loss, but I still can't help but be proud of how these young ladies compete and just don't fold.

1/16/2014

239] You might have noticed that my life, the little one I have, revolves around basketball this time of the year. We lost 52-40 to Itasca last night at their place. Yes, we did it with five players again. Great defensive effort, we just couldn't put the ball in the hole enough.

Practice starts in about an hour; I'm wondering how we should go about it. I know they are tired and a little beat up, so we'll see if we can just ease into it and try to get some work done. We also have to start prepping for a four-hour road trip on Saturday to Northland CTC in Thief River Falls. They are the best team in our conference and nationally ranked. We really have to find a way to survive this one and get back after the rest of the conference.

240] I am definitely impressed about how hard these players are working and how unified they are in their effort to make good things happen, in the face of the adversity of playing with five players. I am also struggling with fear and guilt. I know they all want to do this and they are dedicated, but a part of me has to wonder if it is all worth it. I really worry about their overall health and pray nobody gets hurt. This is true with any team, but it just seems that the worries I have are even more intense when you are running with only five.

1/17/2014

241] I am 54 years old and I will be 55 in April. I say this because it might be the reason for the influx of e-mails I have been receiving lately. I have received advertising or e-mails from AARP, car Leasing companies, cruise lines, retirement planners, and medical advertisements for joint replacements. I get those because of the age thing, but I have also received inquiries from specialized dating services — services that cater to dating Asians, Blacks, and even a cougar dating sight. Maybe my wife has other plans and she has been signing me up to soften the blow. Still doesn't make sense, though; I have been married to the same Caucasian woman, who is one year younger than me, for the past 32 years.

242] It is about 9:00 p.m. and I am in my office waiting for our team laundry to finish drying so it is ready for tomorrow morning. We are leaving at 7:00 a.m. to go to Thief River Falls, MN to play Northland CTC. [See # 239]

After practice this afternoon we had a serious discussion about how we are doing and how we are handling this playing with five players thing. I really had to explain to them that I am sincere about these feelings of fear and guilt about playing with only five players. I do struggle with this, and I wanted them to know it. I also wanted them to tell me if each one of them thought it was worth it. I asked them if all the physical and emotional grind of playing through 14 games and possibly play-offs with just five players is worth it. The answer was a resounding yes!

They are excited about the challenge and going forward. I am still going to continue to pray that we stay healthy and this all turns out to be a great story. All I can tell you right now is this is a great bunch of young ladies and they have a great work mentality. So far, despite everything, they just keep coming to practice every day and go to work. On game days they seem to put the aches and pains to the side and compete for 40 minutes or whatever it takes.

I really hope they have nothing but fond memories of this season down the road; I know I will. It is like that line in that movie about the hotel in India: "Everything will be all right in the end, and if it is not all right, it is not the end."

243] Before I forget, I want you to know who these ladies are I have been talking about. We have one sophomore: Courtney Wirtanen, a 5'6" forward from Hibbing, MN, who will be going to medical school at the University of Minnesota Duluth. Our other four players are all freshman. Our point guard is Christina Wickingson, 5'2", from Drummond, WI. Christina is a ball of energy and has a motor that never stops; she is going to be a good player when she stops being so hard on herself. Our two guard is Danielle Bruns from Nashwauk, MN. Danni is 5'7" and came to us this fall from Itasca CC. She became eligible after Fall Semester. She has been a Godsend and an instant starter. Taylor Martin is 5'10" F/C from Alden in southern Minnesota. Taylor has been rock solid all year and is probably our best player. Now she has to step up and provide even more. Ashlyn Norman, from Hibbing, MN, rounds out the five. She is our Center and is 5'9" tall. Ashlyn did not finish her high school career playing basketball. I don't know how they let her out of the program. She is a great kid, a good student, and the ultimate team player. She had a slow start to the season but has led us in scoring and rebounding in our last five games and was the Conference Player of the Week last week.

They have bonded together to form a very special group and I am hoping are destined to complete a special season. I would be remiss if I didn't mention Arianna Zapata. Arianna is a sophomore from Orr, MN, that was our starting shooting guard and our best three-point shooter. Arianna had a knee injury in our 10th game of the season and is scheduled for reconstructive knee surgery later this month. She is definitely missed on the floor but continues to attend most practices and games and supports us anyway she can.

244] I was watching the news tonight and when Adam Clark came on to do the weather, he gave an in depth explanation of how the Polar Vortex is dropping south again and we will have extremely cold temperatures again next week.

I have may have mentioned this before, but I am 54 years old, and I have lived in Minnesota since the summer of 1975. I have been an avid weather watcher; why is this the first winter I have ever heard of the Polar Vortex? This is the second time this winter it has been a big deal—how did I miss this along the way? I still am just getting use to the European and American models for predicting weather and still have yet to master the El Niña and El Niño thing; now they throw this Polar Vortex tidbit at us!

1/19/2014

245] We made it through the Northland game yesterday. They won by a comfortable margin. We played okay, competitive for the most part. The key thing was nobody got hurt, and we now have all week to get ready to play at Fond Du Lac on Friday.

I love the public address guy at Northland; he has a great voice and has done a very professional job for years. Yesterday, though, he said something in the pre-game introductions that bothered me a little. When he started to introduce, he called my team a "Courageous" five young ladies from Hibbing, MN. I would say tough, but I don't think they should be called "Courageous," even though there are only five of them, for playing in a basketball game. Soldiers are courageous; people battling cancer and other terminal diseases are courageous; astronauts are courageous; firemen and police officers are courageous; people working in bomb squads are courageous. Our group of five young ladies should be commended for playing through a basketball game with only five players, but please don't go as far as calling it courageous; they are having fun playing a game.

246] I visited with Chet Engelman after our game. Chet retired from coaching at Northland shortly after I started my college coaching career. I always enjoy seeing him up there and catching up.

I started out our conversation, picking on him as usual, trying to get one up before he started in on me. I told him he must be tougher than I thought because I was sure this winter's weather would have killed him by now! He responded matter of fact, and told me that he had five heart attacks in the past year and he has a heart surgery scheduled for February. Chet explained that his surgeon was going to put a ball joint in his Aorta so it would operate correctly. He also laughed and said the doctor told him that would be the last time they would see him. If the surgery works they won't have to see him again; if the surgery doesn't work, nobody will see him again. I would have to call Chet "Courageous"!

1/27/2014

247] So we played Fond Du Lac on Friday. I was a part of something I have never experienced as a player or a coach, until now.

We started the game with five players, as we have done for our past seven games. Despite not shooting well, we were up by six points at halftime. Taylor Martin had three fouls, but other than that we were in good shape. Not to take the anticipation out of it but we ended up losing the game 72-63. The end result isn't the story here; it is how we got there.

Taylor fouled out with about 15:30 to play in the second half. We played the next five minutes 4 on 5. Danni Bruns fouled out with about 9:20 to play. Now we were going 3 on 5. With a little over four minutes to play, Courtney Wirtanen fouled out. So, for the next four [+] minutes, Ashlyn Norman and Christina Wickingson went 2 on 5.

I'm not exactly sure of the score, but I know we were still ahead by 3 or 4 points when we went to four players. Christina and Ashlyn did not relinquish the lead until there was about 1:20 to play in the game. Fond Du Lac finally started to cherry pick us; they left one player to stay down on their offensive end so they could just throw the ball down to her if they got a rebound on the defensive end. We tried to counter and leave Ashlyn at half court and let Christina go 1 on 4. Eventually, the slipper fell off and, according to the score, we lost.

A lot of people keep saying they can't believe how well we are doing with "only" five players. I am getting tired of hearing the term, "only" five players. When I see these young ladies on the floor for a game or practice, I don't see "only" five players. I just see a group of extremely united, dedicated, motivated and resilient young women.

I don't know what the future holds for each one of them, but I know they will be successful at whatever comes their way. I also, feel bad for anyone who will expect or need them to back down, because I know they won't.

248] Carrie Pearson, one of the secretaries in the mail/copy room at Hibbing Community College, has taken to calling me "Trouble" over the past few years. I'm pretty sure she does this in jest for the most part. There are times when I'm definitely deserving of the name.

Today, and I think she had something to do with it or we have a very intelligent copy machine, I was put in my place by the copy machine. I have had cooperation problems with the same machine in the past, maybe something to do with the user, but this was over the top. I was about to load the copier to copy off a test. Before I even touched the machine, the display screen lit up and started flashing the message, "A malfunction has been detected; copying not allowed." I hadn't even touched the copier and it called me a "malfunction." That just seems a little harsh.

I reported this to Carrie; she seemed to be amused—probably was because she laughed at me. I know you can file a complaint about a fellow employee, but can you file harassment charges on a copy machine?

1/29/2014

249] I was reading today's Duluth News Tribune, for those of you who do not partake, that is a newspaper. They are about 1 1/2 feet long and about 10 inches wide. They print them every day and put news items, advertising, and other daily information in them. Usually they are separated into sections such as National News, Local News, Sports, Entertainment, and Want Ads. You hold them in your hands and turn the pages as you read through them. My favorite places to read them are at the table, in my recliner, and on the toilet. If you haven't experienced this lately, put down your phone or iPad and go out and buy one. They cost anywhere from 75 cents for a weekday paper to about $3 for a Sunday paper.

Back to today's news; both articles were in the Sports Section. One of the articles was about the newly-formed Labor Union, the CAPA, College Athletes' Player Association. I can't wait to see where this leads. As a coach, I think it would be very interesting having to deal with players who are in an organized labor union. I can see it now; demands for shorter practices, more games and I'm sure more meal money on the road, maybe even two to a room instead of four when we stay overnight.

The second news item was about how much marketing is being done around the Super Bowl hype, concerning marijuana. One shop in Seattle is selling a Cannabis strain they are calling "Beast Mode." Another shop is selling blue and green cupcakes laced with marijuana. Shops in Denver are selling blue and orange bongs and glass pipes. There are t-shirts being sold nationwide marketing Super Bowl Forty-Eight as the "Bud Bowl," "Pack-A-Bowl," and my personal favorite, the "Stoner Bowl." I'm disappointed that we won't see national advertising for marijuana sales during the broadcast. I'm not a pot smoker, but I do love unique Super Bowl commercials. I wonder if the marketing powers of the NFL saw this coming when the two largest U.S. cities with legalized recreational marijuana use qualified teams for this year's Super Bowl. I would to think the NFL is not sanctioning any of this marketing, but they are a huge money-making machine. If Jerry Jones, owner of the Cowboys, starts lobbying the Texas Legislature to approve recreational marijuana use, we'll all know something is up.

May be the NFL executives are into the marijuana thing already. That would explain the decision to put an outdoor Super Bowl in New Jersey in the middle of winter. I know a lot of decisions, good and bad, are made around bong circles.

2/2/2014

250] Well, we played our rematch with Fond Du Lac yesterday. Nice turn of events; nobody fouled out and nobody got hurt. We were able to keep our five players on the court the whole 40 minutes and the result was a 62-57 win.

I am always happy when these ladies get a win. It is a great feeling when they get one! Lord knows how hard they work for it.

251] I am looking forward to watching the Super Bowl later today. I really do not have an emotional attachment and I don't gamble, so nothing is at stake. I just want to see a good game and enjoy the commercials.

2/3/2014

252] Worst Super Bowl ever! Lopsided, right from the start. Whoever coined the phrase "Defense, wins championships" was proven right, again.

I hate to admit it, but I ended up switching back and forth to HGTV and watching *Hawaii Life* and *Beachfront Properties*. I must have dozed off in my chair before halftime, because I missed Bruno Mars' concert performance. Some people I talked to today said that he did a great show.

I did wake-up right before the start of the second half and had hope that Denver would get it going in the second half. Being a Minnesotan and somewhat of a Vikings fan, it was painful to watch Percy Harvin return the kick-off for a touchdown.

If anybody asks me what my Super Bowl Forty-Eight highlight was, I'd have to say, the Chrysler commercial, featuring Bob Dylan. Like I said, worst Super Bowl ever!

253] Yesterday, I heard back from Jansina at Rivershore Books. She is almost done with the edit on my first book, *Random Thoughts of a Stupid Man*. She has agreed to republish the book.

I can't explain how excited I am to have it back in circulation, after the debacle I went through with 2 Moon Press.

If you are reading this book, I hope you are enjoying it. If so, consider picking up a copy of my first book, if you haven't already done so. It will help you make more sense out of what you have been reading in this book.

2/4/2014

254] I was reading another article about the freshman co-ed at the University of Minnesota-Duluth that suffered a severe case of frostbite earlier this winter. The article was about her being moved to a different hospital. The mother of the girl talked about her daughter seeing her hands for the first time since her surgeries.

If you haven't heard this story, I'll try to catch you up. Earlier this winter the girl had been out drinking with some friends. She was dropped off in front of where she lived and was found the next morning on the porch, where she had spent the night in sub-zero temperatures. She ended up with severe frostbite and through multiple surgeries had all of her fingers and parts of both feet amputated. I believe the young lady is a nineteen-year-old freshman.

Having raised two children and being a college instructor and coach, this sad story has hit me on several levels, and I have followed the story closely. I know most college kids drink. I know a lot of questionable choices are made in their lives. I am not here to tell you I was any smarter than them when I was in college. I just hope people, especially college students and teenagers, take notice of stories like this.

No matter what choices are made, good and bad, make sure everyone is safe, healthy, and secure when you are done at the end of a night. Don't leave anyone alone and unaccounted for. I get the Superman and Superwoman mentality, but I'm pretty sure alcohol and sub-zero temperatures will win every time. I pray that we don't have to hear more stories like this for kids to understand and never forget to take care of each other.

2/6/2014

255] We had another basketball game last night at home against Northland. They came in 17 and 1 overall, undefeated in the division, and ranked 6th in the nation. We have been playing very well lately and are still going with five players. We had our moments of success but ended up losing 88-44. Nobody fouled out and we competed hard all night.

I know the game took a physical toll on us and I hope we recover in time for a key division game with Itasca on Saturday. Today, we'll just watch film and we'll get after it again tomorrow.

2/7/2014

256] Our basketball team could be faced with an even tougher task tomorrow. Taylor Martin, our leading scorer and rebounder, needed to sit out most of practice today with back spasms. She'll be game time decision tomorrow afternoon, we have a shoot around at 9:00 and we play at 1:00.

We have one girl on our eligibility roster who has not played since before Christmas and could possibly help us out. We'll check on that tonight. Otherwise we have two other options if Taylor is not good to go tomorrow. We can forfeit the game, or we can insert Taylor in the starting line-up — you have to start a game with five — then we can take her off the floor and go 4 on 5 the rest of the game.

I presented both scenarios to our team tonight and, to no surprise, they were unanimously in favor of option number two, start Taylor, take her off the floor, and go 4 on 5. I've been with these ladies since October and watched the five of them go to work and compete every day since Christmas with five players, and I still can't tell you how physically and mentally tough they are. They prove it every time they step on the court. When I hit my knees tonight, I am definitely praying that Taylor comes in tomorrow feeling a lot better. I normally don't try to get God involved in sports. I have never been convinced He is a fan and if He is, I don't think He should favor one team over another. Tonight I am going to make an exception, because these young ladies are deserving of any help they can get.

2/9/2014

257] Great day yesterday; we beat Itasca 55-44. Taylor gutted it out and played very well, point guard had only three turnovers, and nobody fouled out.

After the game, my wife and I had the perfect date night. We went to a mystery dinner theater at the Discovery Center. The mystery was called *A Night at the Clueseum*. It was a makeshift mystery designed after the board game, Clue. We went with some other couples and had a great time.

We were back from the dinner around 7:00, and Pam thought it would be fun to go seethe Abba tribute band that was playing at the high school auditorium. I couldn't hide the fact that this idea didn't thrill me. She, thank God, opted for going by herself and meeting some friends at the concert. No guilt trip involved; she said I could stay home and watch the Olympics on television.

Pam went to the concert and had a great time. I enjoyed watching the Olympics and did not have to listen to Abba's greatest hits. Now that I look at that in print, it just doesn't seem right to have Abba and greatest hits in the same sentence. Anyway, like I said before: perfect date night.

2/12/2014

258] I read Jay Baer's report today on Twitter accounts in the U.S. I was surprised to read that only 17 million people in the U.S. use Twitter. That means that there are roughly 297 million people in the U.S. who don't. I am proud to say, I am one of the non-users. I am also one of the 1 in every 13 people who know about Twitter and choose not to use it.

If these statistics are true, then why do avid Twitter users think it is such a big deal? Do they know that 297 million people in the U.S. couldn't care less?

2/14/2014

259] Happy Valentine's Day! We have a basketball game tonight at Mesabi, so once again, I am abandoning my wife on Valentine's Day. In 34 years of coaching basketball, I'm pretty sure this has happened several times, but there is still some sense of guilt.

We did Valentines last night. We started with a romantic dinner: Burger Night at the Elks Club. Afterwards, we went to a concert at the college, Davina and the Vagabonds. Out of all the musical acts that have performed at the college auditorium, they are still my favorite.

I also left gifts for Pam in the sunroom at the house: a card, flowers, a large teddy bear, and a bottle of Rumchata. The teddy bear didn't go over real big, but I think the card, flowers, and Rumchata were well received. Despite Pam's warnings of not spending as much as I did last year, I think I did okay.

We didn't have any guests eating breakfast this morning at our Bed & Breakfast, so we were able to go to the Sportsmen's Café for breakfast. Pam loves the pancakes there. Personally, I think they are laced with some pleasure-producing drug, because they are addictive. It is a good thing we don't have the opportunity to eat there often.

Before we went to breakfast, I was able to finish shoveling for the fourth time in the last two days! This winter has been brutal; we have been setting records all winter for snowfall and sub-zero temperatures. Pam and I are planning a trip to Florida for the second week of March; there is hope! When I came back in from shoveling, Pam surprised me with a very nice card and several boxes of theater candy. Great gift; don't tell anyone, but we sneak candy into the movie theater. We buy the popcorn, you can't beat real theater popcorn, but candy is candy. I can't see paying $3.50 for a box of candy you can get at the grocery store for a dollar.

If I ever get caught, I will be hard pressed not to tell the usher that my wife is also hiding a bottle of iced tea in her purse. I have to admit, it feels good to confess to this criminal behavior, but let's just keep it between you and me.

260] I was listening to the radio this afternoon, and the announcers on WEVE were discussing the ways Valentine's Day is celebrated in different countries. They said that in Japan the men do nothing. It is all about them; the women buy the presents, make reservations, pay for dinner, etc. Are Japanese men that much smarter than American men? How did they manage to get a holiday that honors them? We have a day that is close, but you have to be a father. This one is for all males, so fathers would get two days a year; how great is that! I wonder how American women have managed to keep this concept from sneaking into our culture. As soon as I have more time on my hands, I might have to start working on a plan to promote this idea.

2/16/2014

261] Our basketball team, "The Iron Five" according to the Hibbing Daily Tribune, is down to one game left in the regular season. We lost to at Mesabi on Friday night, 77-62. Very physical game; our point guard, Christina Wickingson, fouled out with about four minutes to go and it was tough sledding from there. We came out of it a little beat up but healthy.

My players put teddy bears on the bench before the game last night. I don't know if it was to keep me company during the game or to make it look like we had substitutes. If the purpose was to create a bench, those bears were worthless. Our starters outscored the Mesabi starters 62-36, but according to the stat sheet, our bench got outscored 41-0. That is the worst our bench has done all year.

Yesterday we played Vermilion at home in a game that would cost us a chance to make the post-season tournament if we lost it. I didn't allow the teddy bears on the bench; I thought we would be better served without them.

We had a three-point lead when Courtney Wirtanen fouled out with a little over two minutes to play. That left us with the four remaining players, all freshmen, to ice away the game. They did a great job and we won 58-54.

Next, we travel to Rainy River on Wednesday, and a win there could seal the fourth and final spot in the Regional Tournament. If we do win, we will still have to wait until the results of the Itasca vs. Mesabi game on Saturday to finalize our fate. If we lose on Wednesday, the standings will become very dicey and the fourth-place team might have to be determined by a coin toss.

262] I have really been enjoying watching the Winter Olympics; I always have. I really get a thrill out of watching athletes compete at the highest level. There is something about watching people compete, when you know that they have prepared for most of their waking hours over the past four years to prepare for that single moment to perform. ABC's Wide World of Sports nailed it years ago with the line, "Spanning the globe to bring you the joy of victory and the agony of defeat."

When I watch the Ski Jumping events, I am overwhelmed with fond memories of my dad. First of all because of all the stories he would tell about him and his friends ski jumping off the edges of the Iron Ore pits by Pool Location, outside of Hibbing, MN, where he grew up. Secondly, because when my dad was alive, the only two sporting events he would sit down and watch on television with me were the Army vs. Navy football game and Ski Jumping. Other than that, the only television I remember him watching was, 60 Minutes, The Sunday Morning Show, and the local 10:00 news. I am not a 60 Minutes fan, but I am an avid watcher of the Sunday Morning Show, and I rarely miss the 10:00 news.

263] I know that there has been concern that the American athletes wear apparel made in the U.S. during the Olympics, but if the sweaters that were worn during the opening ceremonies are the best we can do, we either need another fashion designer before 2016 or we better consider looking outside the country. I have been watching quite a bit of the broadcasts and I haven't no-

ticed any of the athletes wearing those sweaters since the opening ceremonies. It has been warm in Sochi, but I don't think that
is the reason. The athletes probably put them away and will
break them out the next time they are invited to an ugly sweater
party — or maybe they were donated to homeless Russians.

264] I know they are not doing so well, but I also enjoy watching
the American Men's Curling Team. I have a vested interest, like
many others from northeastern Minnesota, because all the team
members are from around here; Hibbing, Chisholm, Gilbert,
and Duluth. The team's skip, John Shuster, a Chisholm, MN
native, is an ex-player of mine. He played baseball here at Hibbing Community College in the early 2000s. John was already
an avid curler at that time. His sophomore year, he had to miss
the first part of our spring baseball trip to compete at the world
championships in Utica, NY. John flew into Pensacola, FL when
he was done and joined us for the rest of our games in Alabama.

The first day he was with us, we were playing at Jefferson Davis
in Brewton, Al. Players and coaches on their team had seen him
curl on television and wanted to meet him after the game. We
got beat handily by Jefferson Davis, but after the game John and
some of our other players that curled gave a curling clinic in the
parking lot outside of the stadium to their players and coaches.
We had just gotten our butts kicked on the baseball field and
within minutes our guys were being treated like rock stars.

John has now curled in three Olympics and his team won a
bronze medal the first time around. He is a great ambassador
for the sport, and we are proud to say he is a Hibbing CC alum-
nus.

265] I am going to stop writing now and go home to take a nap.
I need to prepare for another snowstorm and the shoveling and
snow blowing that goes with it. We are supposed to get another 5 to 8 inches tonight. This is really getting old! Fortunately,
tomorrow is President's Day and we don't have classes. We do
have basketball practice at 6:00; maybe my players would en-
tertain something different for conditioning? I doubt it, though;
they would probably want to get paid for work study hours.
I'm pretty sure it would be illegal to pay them for shoveling
my sidewalks and driveway. I'll have to check on that. We are

supposed to get a bigger storm next weekend. Around here, they call them Alberta Clippers. What did we ever do to Alberta, Canada that they insist on sending us several snowstorms every year? I would hate to see how big next week's storm is if our men's and women's hockey teams beat the Canadians this week at the Olympics.

2/17/2014

266] So much for 5 to 8 inches of snow; I would say more like 10 to 12 inches. I spent five hours today shoveling and blowing snow.

When I am shoveling, my mind tends to wander; neither is an uncommon event in my life. Today my mind wandered to Florida and then to trying to put a game plan together for the Rainy River game on Wednesday. It seemed as though every time my mind and body rejoined each other, it was still snowing and I was still shoveling. About four hours into my snow removal duties, I was done with round one. Round two would have to come later in the afternoon, if it quit snowing.

I was standing on the back porch admiring my work when that dreaded beeping noise could be heard coming around the corner. Sure enough, it was my nemesis: the city snowplow driver. It really doesn't matter which corner he comes from; we live on a corner lot. We have calendar parking in Hibbing, so some days we get a pardon if there are cars parked on our side of the street. Today was not my lucky day; there were no cars parked on our side of the road. The plow came by and threw about three feet of snow and ice chunks across the end of my driveway, the corner sidewalk entries, and the two boulevard sidewalks.

I am convinced the snowplow drivers send out scouts to see when you are done with your snow removal. The scout lets them know and then they come plow you in. One of the younger drivers seems to exhibit some sense of guilt. If you are outside when he comes by, he doesn't establish eye contact. There is an older driver that seems to actually enjoy plowing people in; driveways, sidewalks, parked cars — you name it, he seems to enjoy it.

I realize that city snow removal is crucial, but I tire of this ongoing battle. If we throw snow in the road, we can be fined by the city. If the snowplows throw snow onto our property, there is no recourse; just doesn't seem fair.

I am aware that bullying has become a major focus of concern in schools, workplaces, and even the NFL. Is there any chance that household owners could band against the city and bring up bullying accusations on the snowplow drivers? I seriously doubt it, but I do think young bullies should consider a future career as snowplow drivers. I'm sure they would find it an enjoyable occupation.

Back to that Alberta Clipper thing [#265], the Canadians definitely kicked our butt with this one. We Americans got our revenge this afternoon, though. Meryl Davis and Charlie White took the gold medal in Ice Dancing and defeated the Canadian pair, Virtue and Moir, to do it! We'll see how the rest of the week goes. We have another Alberta Clipper due later in the week and the U.S. men's and women's teams might be playing Canada in gold medal games.

2/17/2014

267] My wife and I went to the movie theater yesterday [yes, I snuck some candy in] and saw the movie *Philomena*. Great movie; made me proud to be an ex-Catholic and for the most part, a democrat. [Sarcasm Alert: in case you haven't seen the movie.] We both really did enjoy the movie, though.

2/18/2014

268] The streak is over. In northeastern Minnesota we had 62 straight days where sub-zero temperatures were recorded at some time during the day. That streak came to an end yesterday; yay! Our high temperature actually hit the upper 30s. I'm pretty sure those Canadians are going to make sure we haven't seen the end of winter though.

2/19/2014

269] No magic in International Falls tonight; we lost to Rainy River 61-49. We didn't shoot it very well and two of Rainy River's players had excellent nights. Luckily Itasca lost to Northland, so we are still clinging to that fourth and final spot for the region play-offs.

We have completed our regular season games and have a bye on Saturday. Now all we can do is sit back and wait for the rest of the league to finish playing on Saturday.

If Itasca beats Mesabi, we are done and Itasca will go to Regions. If Itasca loses, we will be in a two- or three-way tie for fourth and the league will conduct a coin toss on Sunday to see which team goes to the Regional Tournament. We'll take tomorrow off from practice and come back in on Friday and start preparing as if we are going to Regions next week.

2/20/2014

270] Today, Alberta Canada sent us another clipper. Ten inches of snow so far and twenty-five mile an hour winds. Why couldn't those darn Canadians just be happy enough with beating the U.S. women in the hockey gold medal game? This is just downright mean.

271] I was supposed to be going to Solon Springs, WI tonight to recruit a basketball player. Her game has been cancelled. I am really hoping I can still get over there one more time. She would be a very good addition to next year's squad.

Tonight, I'll just have to stay home and work on round one of shoveling out.

2/21/2014

272] Woke up this morning to about six more inches of snow and some serious snowdrifts from all the wind. Also, a rare event, the ticker on the bottom of the television screen listed Hibbing Community College: CLOSED TODAY. I believe this is the third time in my sixteen years here that this has happened, and wouldn't you know it, it is Friday and I have no classes anyway. More time to work on shoveling out! Hopefully I can get it done and the plows don't come by until tonight.

Those Canadians are relentless; the worst Alberta Clipper of the year and they beat the U.S. men's hockey team in the semi-final today. I hope they back-off now.

2/22/2014

273] Good news; the sun is shining. Bad news; it is nine degrees below zero. Those Canadians dropped the Polar Vortex on us again, and the plows came by the house this morning. I am not going to jump into this day right away. I'll go to the barber for a haircut and then go home and start shoveling again.

274] Great time at the barber shop; bunch of guys just being guys. The barber shop is one of my favorite places for social networking. The three main topics of conversation were the weather, the Olympics, and snowplow drivers.

Hibbing is an Iron Range town and hockey is king, so there was a lot of lamenting about the demise of our two U.S. hockey teams. I was also surprised to see how many guys admitted to watching the Women's Figure Skating.

The weather discussion turned quickly to the battles with snowplow drivers. It just so happened that we had one in our midst. When it was his turn in the chair, one of the barbers jokingly held a straight razor to his ear and threatened to cut it off, if all of our demands were not met. Demands were verbalized; it wasn't near as scary as the uprising in the Ukraine and we were joking around, but I can't help but think this guy might have a few nightmares later. Who would have ever guessed a barber and a small group of men could possibly have such an impact on the future of public snow removal in a northern Minnesota town. I don't think you will be reading about this in the news, but I'm glad I was there to witness it and participate in such a monumental event.

2/23/2014

275] It is about 12:45 a.m. and I can't sleep, so I'll do some writing; maybe it will help me clear my head so I can sleep.

No doubt why I can't sleep; we have the draw for which team gets the fourth position in the Region 13 NJCAA Women's basketball tournament. Mesabi beat Itasca and Rainy River beat Fond Du Lac on Saturday, so Hibbing, Itasca, and Rainy River finished in a three-way tie for fourth. The league commissioner will conduct a conference call at 12:00 noon to decide who gets the fourth spot. I know it is all out of my hands now, but I still can't sleep. It is really eating at me that we have played a 27-game regular season and it now comes down to a coin toss to determine the number four seed in the tournament. After playing all twelve division games with five players, it just doesn't seem right to determine the post-season fate of these young ladies with a coin toss. We have already done a team vote, and my players want me to call heads if I get to make the call. I have put my faith in them all year, so I will call heads.

276] This afternoon Pam and I went to watch our nephew play hockey in Eveleth at the Hippodrome. Pretty cool; I have only attended two hockey games in the Hippodrome. I went with my dad in 1975 and saw the University of Minnesota Gophers play an exhibition game against the U.S. Olympic team, and in 1977 I saw Ely High School play Eveleth. The Hippodrome hosted its first hockey game on January 1, 1922. In the 1920s the Hippodrome was referred to as the "Madison Square Garden of the Northland."

My nephew plays for the Ely Mite team. This was the first time we got to see him play. Ely lost to Virginia twenty-something to one. Logan had the lone goal for Ely. I am sure those kids will soon forget the results of the game, but I hope they never forget they had the opportunity to play in such a historic hockey venue.

277] When Pam and I got back from Eveleth, I headed over to Chisholm, MN to watch Chisholm and Ely play their last regular season game of the boys' high school basketball season.

Most seasons, this would be no big deal, but tonight was different. This was the last game that Bob McDonald, the Chisholm coach, would be coaching in Roels Gym. Bob is retiring after 59 years of coaching. He has coached in Chisholm for 53 years and has over 1,000 victories. The victory total is not the focal point here. It is nothing short of incredible that this guy has coached for 59 years!

I can only marvel at this feat. I am contemplating retiring after next year, which will mark thirty-four years. Bob has coached longer than I have been alive. This just boggles my mind. I think it is safe to assume that Bob's coaching longevity will never be duplicated.

278] 2:30 a.m.: I'll try to go back to bed again now. First, I'll say a few more prayers. I know I have said before that I don't think God is a sports fan, but if He does have any involvement in this draw tomorrow, all I can say is: GO CARDS!

279] 11:00 a.m.: I went to church this morning. Thought I'd check-in one more time before the draw. It can't hurt, right?

280] 12:30 p.m: That was a heartbreaker! It took just a couple of minutes to determine our fate. Me and the Rainy River and Itasca coaches and Athletic Directors sat there on the phones and listened while the commissioner and a member of the league executive committee conducted the draw. Three pieces of paper in a hat, one name drawn to see who was going to the Region Tournament. No drum roll, no envelope, just silence and then the announcement: Rainy River…and that was it.

I passed the bad news on to my players, and we will meet on Monday to clean out lockers and turn in equipment. Every season comes to an end sometime. Whether we have a good season or bad one, it comes down to clean-out day. This is not going to be easy; this season was special and this group of young ladies was special. I will try to revisit this later when I come up with the right words, if I ever do. I look forward to seeing them on Monday, but right now I really don't know what I can tell them to make it hurt any less. I have always thought that athletic participation and competition teaches us many life lessons, and this season was definitely no exception.

281] Proof that life moves forward, no matter what happens. I have to go home and remove snow from our roof, and I have to be back up here at the gym at 8:00 for spring volleyball practice. Three of my basketball players are volleyball players. Later this afternoon the softball team has practice; three of my basketball players are softball players.

We all have things to move on to, but I will feel a loss when 3:10 p.m. rolls around on Monday and I am not looking at those five young ladies standing on the baseline of the basketball court waiting to start practice.

2/24/2014

284] A couple of weeks ago Michael Sam, an NFL prospect from the University of Missouri, announced he was gay. The media has created a big buzz over this, saying that he has the chance to be the first openly gay athlete in one of the four major professional sports in the U.S. Tonight, Jason Collins played in an NBA game for the Brooklyn Nets. Jason Collins publically announced he was gay a year ago. He has already played in the NBA for 12 or 13 years, but this was his first game since making the announcement. So, technically Michael Sam will not be the first.

Why is the media making such a big deal over this? I can't see what all the fuss is about; are we really that archaic? We have had athletes in major sports that are openly political activists, Christians, Jewish, Catholics, and Muslims. Not to mention openly democratic and/or republican. Steve Young was openly Mormon, there are openly Japanese athletes playing in the major leagues, and even Cuban defectors. Joe Dimaggio was Italian-American and openly married to Marilyn Monroe. Renaldo Nehemiah was definitely openly a track athlete when he played for the 49ers. Bo Jackson couldn't make up his mind about baseball or football, but he was open about it. Magic Johnson tested HIV positive. I think Herschel Walker and Willie Gault were both openly ballet dancers when they played in the NFL. Nancy Lieberman was openly female when she played in the USBL and with the Washington Generals. David Wells and John Kruk were openly overweight when they played major league base-ball. I am pretty sure Terry Bradshaw was pretty open about not being very smart when he played with the Steelers. Joe Namath wore pantyhose in a commercial when he played for the Jets. There are players in the NHL that are openly black. George Blanda was openly old when he played for the Oak-land Raiders. Michael Jordan openly smoked cigars, golfed, and gambled. Justin Morneau was openly Canadian when he played for the Twins. Donald Driver was on *Dancing with the Stars*, and the list goes on and on.

My point is that somehow we have managed to get over all this openness in the past and major sports have thrived. Hopefully we will see the day that stories such as Michael Sam's and Jason Collin's will not really be newsworthy. Besides, I think that the media and the powers that be in our four major sports should be more concerned with the athletes that are still in the closet; the ones that don't admit to being alcoholics, drug addicts, rap-ists, performance-enhancing drug users, drunk drivers, mur-derers, or wife beaters. These are the guys that scare me and need to come out.

2/26/2014

285] I went recruiting in Duluth last night. On the drive down I was passed by a KIA Soul. Quick survey: which vehicle is ug-lier, a KIA Soul or a Scion SUV?

286] A lot of people worry about germs and proper hygiene. Many of us wash our hands several times a day, and we make sure to sneeze and cough through a bent elbow.

If this is true, what is so magical about a bar of soap? Can you think of anything else that people are willing to rub on their feet, butt, crotch, armpits, and then their face and not even think twice about it? Some people even share the same bar of soap; family members, teammates, roommates, etc.

287] We are supposed to get snow flurries tonight and a low temperature of 25 degrees below zero. One week from tonight, my wife and I are flying out of Duluth, MN and going to Or-lando, FL to spend a week. It will be about a three hour flight, hopefully—and this is not so farfetched, it will be about 100 degrees warmer in Florida. I'm getting warmer just thinking about it.

2/27/2014

288] I was thinking about Random Thought #286; I guess a towel would be a possibility, but we usually don't share those nearly as much.

289] I finished the season-ending personal interviews with my basketball players. All four freshmen are returning next year. We will also have Amber Zapata back, so technically we return five starters; nice! If recruiting continues to go well, we might be on to something for the 2014-2015 basketball season.

3/3/2014

290] The temperature has been pushing thirty degrees below zero the last couple of nights. Pam and I are leaving for Florida on Wednesday night. That flight out of Duluth can't happen soon enough.

291] I think I watched the Academy Awards last night, from the beginning to the end for the first time in my life. How great was Ellen Degeneres as the host? The pizza delivery and her selfie with all those actors and actresses were hilarious.

292] It has been just a little over a week now since our basketball season ended. The numbness is starting to wear off. I think what has made it so hard to absorb is that the season did not end on the court. In the 33 years I have been coaching and every season I ever played, always ended with a win or a loss on the court or field. Our 2013-14 basketball season ended in my office on a conference call. That is just not how any coach or player wants to end a season; it is really an empty, anti-climatic finish.

We have a state coaches meeting later this week. I am presenting a proposal to change our tie-breaking procedure for play-off positions, so there will be a play-off to break ties in the future. These kids work too hard to have their fate decided by a draw or a coin flip. We'll see if my coaching cohorts agree.

3/5/2014

293] It is Ash Wednesday today. In my Catholic years, this would have meant the beginning of lent and I would be giving up something I enjoyed doing or eating. Today is a whole different story, and I'm sorry but I can't get the smile off my face. Pam and I are flying out of Duluth today at 5:30 and going to Florida for 10 days. It was 18 degrees below zero last night, and we still have snowbanks piled above my head [I am 6'3" tall].

We'll see what "Random Thoughts" come to mind when I'm walking the beach. I will offer a moment of pause to think about those who couldn't escape northeast Minnesota this year. Okay, that's done; I'm out of here!

3/16/2014

294] Pam and I flew back into Duluth last night; arrived at about 4:30 p.m. Depression officially set in at about 5:45 on the drive back to Hibbing. On Saturday morning we had breakfast on the porch of the Beach Drive Inn Bed and Breakfast, across from the marina in St. Petersburg, Florida, and it was about seventy degrees. We drove to Orlando and flew out at about 1:30 on a gorgeous eighty-degree afternoon. When we touched down in sunny Duluth, MN it was sixteen degrees. My wife, being the purebred northern Minnesota girl she is, was excited to be back in her element. I, on the other hand, was ready to jump the next plane back to Florida.

295] We had a great trip; not quite as much beach time as I would have liked, but all the same, a very enjoyable ten days.

296] Pam did a great job of planning the trip and setting us up for a whirlwind tour of Florida. We started out with one night and the better part of two days on Amelia Island, northeast of Jacksonville.

From there we moved on to St. Augustine. Highlights there included touring Flagler College and attending a Celtic Heritage Fest in the Park and a great dinner at Rhett's downtown.

The next day we drove down to Palm Beach so Pam could tour

the Flagler Museum and the Breakers Hotel. While Pam was at the museum, I went on my own self-guided walking tour of Royal Poinciana Drive and attempt to hang out with the rich and somewhat famous. I found a newsstand, purchased a Sunday Palm Beach Post, and tried to find a bar that would allow me to enter and sit for a while. My first stop was Nick and Johnny's. I ordered a beer, pretended to read the paper, and started people watching. As I watched and listened, I attempted to take a few observational notes on napkins. This is some of what I was able to decipher from my chicken scratch: Sign above the bar: "Don't Chase Anything but Drinks and Dreams!" Three women sitting to my left, I would guess 50 to 60ish, conversing about their latest implants, tucks, and Botox injections. At the end of the bar: three waitresses on a break asked me if they could look at the Want Ads in my paper. I obliged and listened while they read through the "Rich Guys Seeking Female Companionship" section. To my right at the far end of the bar there was a guy that looked like he had just stopped in while jogging through the neighborhood. A little sweaty, but he had a glistening tan. He was surrounded by several women that seemed enamored with anything he had to say. I began to wonder to myself what his deal was, because I noticed he handed a business card to any new woman who stepped up. The three women to my left informed me that he was Palm Beach's most sought-after plastic surgeon. I went back to reading the paper, ordered another beer, and began paying more attention to Brett Staskas, a guitar-playing singer who was playing out in the courtyard. He was outstanding; even made some Bob Dylan covers sound good.

I started thinking it was time to start making my way back to the museum to meet Pam, so I finished my beer and headed up the street. On my walk back, I came by Testa's Sidewalk Café. I noticed there were a couple of spots opened at the bar and asked one of the waitresses if there was open seating. It was my lucky day; she invited me in. I know it wasn't the Flagler Museum, but this turned out to be an important part of Palm Beach history. Testa's was established in 1921 and who knows who had graced this bar over the years. The first guy I talked to, can't remember his name, had to cut our conversation short so he could finish closing a real estate deal on a five and half million dollar condominium. When we revisited our conversation, he explained that he was a real estate broker and asked if I was looking. I told him I was just in town for the afternoon and was actually interested in real estate a little further north, possibly a lake cabin. Turns out, there aren't any cabins in Palm Beach. I started talking to a couple of other guys and they became very interested when I told them I was from northern Minnesota. Their main question was: "Why?" I told them I would love to live down south, but my wife has no interest. They offered to wait at the bar if I would go pick up Pam and bring her back, and they would convince her to move to Florida. I left, went back to the museum, picked up Pam, and we came back to Testa's.

When Pam and I returned, they were waiting for us. Right away they started wining and dining Pam. One of the owners even toured Pam around the bar and told her the history of the place. Pam listened to all of their sales pitches on the benefits of living in Florida, and she gave them her version of the "Explore Minnesota" speech. At some point, Pam went off to the bathroom and these guys told me to drop any dreams of moving south, because it was quite evident to them it wasn't going to happen. When Pam returned, it was time to go. We thanked everyone for their hospitality and we were on our way.

297] On our drive out of Palm Beach, all I could think of was how bizarre my afternoon on Royal Poinciana Way had been. I shouldn't say bizarre; let's just go with interesting. It never ceases to amaze me just how much fun you can have talking to and meeting new people if you just keep your nose out of your cell phone and the headphones off your ears. Some days, I come away feeling a lot smarter because I don't have a smart phone and the phone I do own is usually off.

When I first stepped into Nick & Johnny's, I couldn't help but notice the Rolexes, Armani suits, Gucci shoes and bags, and other apparel people were wearing with logos I had never seen before. The parking lot was a lot different also. At home I'm used to seeing a lot of F-150's, Sierras, Rams, Silverados, and various mini-vans and cross-overs. The parking lot here was full of Jaguars, Bentleys, Escalades, and, on the low end, a couple of

Lexuses. I had walked in, left our Taurus rental at the museum, and I was wearing Tek sandals from L&M Fleet Supply, Dickie cargo shorts from Shopko, Saint John's Bay polo from JC Penney's, reading glasses from the Dollar Store, my Timex Ironman watch, and forty-five dollar wedding band from Wal-Mart. I used to own a better wedding band, but this is my fourth one. The first one had to be cut-off, and I lost two others coaching baseball. It made no sense to keep buying expensive ones, and I have had the cheap one longer than any of the others. The point I was attempting to make is that these people were in a whole different world. I'm not sure if one guy was just trying to jerk me around a little, but he did ask me if Dickie was a new designer.

Despite the culture shock, I had a great time, and I hope the people I met think well of Minnesotans after meeting Pam and me. We gave them a full dose of Minnesota nice!

298] That night we stayed in Port Saint Lucie. I was planning to go see the Mets and the Marlins the next day, and then we were going over to Fort Myers. In the morning we decided we wouldn't have time for me to go to the game, stop and see a friend in Fort Lauderdale, and then make the drive across Alligator Alley. So Pam was extremely happy to skip the game and drive down A1A along the coast and look at mansions. It was a beautiful drive, I got to look at the ocean, and Pam was able to overdose on mansion gawking. We had to cancel dinner plans with our friend in the Miami area but we had a great lunch at Lauderdale by the Beach. We made the drive across Alligator Alley but didn't see a single alligator — just a lot of birds. I thought eastern North Dakota was flat, but it doesn't begin to compare to that stretch of highway. When we got to the coast we went to Marco Island but couldn't find anywhere to stay. We drove back up to Naples and hit the big time; Pam went online and found a great deal at a Red Roof Inn. Don't scoff; it was actually a Red Roof Inn and Suites and there was an IHOP right across the parking lot. We don't have an IHOP within two hours of where we live.

After breakfast the next morning, we drove all over Naples, up and down Gulf Shore Drive, looking for, Millionaire Row. I don't know if we ever found it, but we went through some beautiful neighborhoods and I'm sure they were full of multi-million dollar homes.

299] We stayed in Fort Myers for the next three nights at Kip and Carol Johnson's condominium. Kip and Carol have been coming to Hibbing to stay at our bed & breakfast for the past several years, and they have always said to look them up if we were ever in Florida; who knew?

The first day they took us out to Sanibel Island. We walked the beach and had dinner in a restaurant at the marina. Best Key Lime pie that I had anywhere in Florida. It was also a Godsend they were doing the driving; Pam and I would have never found anywhere on the island to park. Kip and Carol had lived and worked on Sanibel and knew exactly where to go.

The next day Kip and I went to the Twins and Pirates game. I had never been to Hammond Field before and I am a huge baseball fan, so this was a special treat. The Twins look much improved over the past few years; I hope it carries over to a good season when they get back up north. I hope the heaters under Target Field are working and they get to play at home in April. Pam also enjoyed her day; she didn't have to go to a baseball game, and she was able to tour the Henry Ford and Thomas Edison homes and museum. Carol missed all the fun because of a doctor's appointment. At the end of the day, we all went to dinner at Pinchers by the Fort Myers Yacht Club. Carol won't be eating there again, but the rest of us enjoyed it.

On Thursday morning Kip drove Pam and I over to the Fort Myers Beach Marina so Pam and I could take a day a day trip to Key West. Kip and Carol had talked us out of driving through the Keys earlier in the week because it would be easier to take this day trip. The trip is scheduled for three hours down and three hours back, and you get about five hours to tour Key West on your own in between. Sounded like a great deal, on paper. The weather was sunny and warm but…windy. The Gulf was a little rough, so the trip down took about four hours. Once on the island, we did a whirlwind tour of Key West. We toured Harry Truman's Little White House, the Naval Annex, and Hemmingway's House; all good, but I don't like cats and they wander all over the Hemingway House and Gardens. After the touring, we hustled down to the Buoy and took the tourist picture at the southernmost geographical point in the U.S. From there it was the shops and somewhere to eat. Fortunately, Pam is not a huge shopper and she knew she was limited by our forty-pound luggage limit flying on Allegiant Airlines. I did manage to poke my head into Sloppy Joe's, bought a Red Sox t-shirt in the Lazy-Gecko, and had a Daquiri in Flying Monkeys.

The real fun started on the cruise back to Fort Myers. The captain announced that we would be experiencing rough seas on the way, and he would do what he could do to keep the trip as comfortable as possible. There were probably a couple hundred people on the ship, and I would venture to guess the vast majority got sick. The first to go down was anyone who had drank too much or spent too much time in the sun while on the island. We both made it through that round, but it was just a matter of time. The lady sitting across from us asked for a barf bag about an hour into the trip; Pam followed shortly afterward. Somehow, I and the husband of the lady across from us managed to hold it together. I know he didn't look so well and I am sure I didn't either because I know we were both on the verge of losing anything we had eaten for the past few days. I felt bad for the ship stewards; all they did for four hours was hand out empty barf bags and fresh paper towels and collect full barf bags and used paper towels. They also spent a lot of time cleaning up after people who didn't master the use of a barf bag. The cruise back took about four and a half hours. Pam survived and said she was feeling much better when we were back on land. When Kip picked us up, he said that the sunset view on the way back must have been amazing. I'm sure it was, but neither one of us had seen it because you just got sicker if you tried to watch the horizon. Anyway, Key West: been there done that!

300] Friday morning we said our goodbyes to our wonderful hosts and headed up to Saint Petersburg for our last night in Florida. Pam wanted to stop in Sarasota and tour the Ringling Brothers Circus Museum, Art Gallery, and Mansion. I am not going to lie; I was trying to figure out if we had enough time to drop me off in Bradenton and I could go to the Pirates and Phillies game and Pam could do the Ringling Brothers tour. Not happening, so somewhat reluctantly I was along for the ride. Pam nailed this one; as she put it, "FABLIOUSO." I loved it; the circus museums, the mansion, the Art Gallery, the restaurant, all of it! I will admit, though, I didn't spend a lot of time in the clown displays, since I have a clown phobia. Anyway, for whatever it is worth, if you are ever in Sarasota, make a point of stopping at the Ringling Brothers attraction. I can't think of anyone of any age who wouldn't enjoy it.

That evening we arrived in Saint Petersburg and stayed at the Beach Drive Inn Bed and Breakfast right across the street from the Saint Petersburg Marina. Pam wanted to do one more tour: the historic Vinoy Hotel. I was all toured out at this point, but God was with me; the Hotel was right across the street, next to the marina. We took a short trolley ride through downtown Saint Petersburg, figured out where to go for dinner, got dropped off in front of the hotel, and did a self-guided tour; I had snacks in the lobby and Pam read the historic timeline of the hotel that was displayed on the wall of the lobby. We walked down Beach Drive, had a great dinner, and sat out in front of an ice cream parlor and had gelato for dessert. Went back to the Bed and Breakfast and had wine on the porch swing and watched the nearly full moon come up over the Vinoy Hotel. Perfect end to a great vacation.

301] Refer to Random Thought number 294. I'm sitting here in my office at school, somewhat depressed and all alone, just trying to share some closing Random Thoughts with you, if this book ever made it to print and you are still reading it at this point. Spring Break 2014 is over, I am in Hibbing, MN, and school starts again tomorrow morning. When I'm done writing I need to take some notes for my Chapter Five lecture tomorrow for my Wellness class. I hope at least one person notices that I have a tan and asks me what I did over break.

After class I have to drive down to Austin, MN and visit my mom in the hospital before I drive back up to Minneapolis to do some recruiting at the Minnesota Girl's State Basketball Tournament and then go back to Austin to visit with my mom again on the weekend. The plan was just to go to Minneapolis for the week, but my mom gave us all another scare again while Pam and I were on vacation. She had another fall, was put in the hospital, and had to have a couple of toes removed as a result of an infection from her diabetes and an infection from a recent surgery. She has now been moved to the same rehabilitation center in Austin where my sister Terri works and my mom spent time in this past summer. My sisters Lisa, Stacie, and Terri have been dealing with this most of the time Pam and I have been gone. I called my mom to let her know I'm coming down tomorrow. She seemed excited and wants to hear all about our trip. I know there is nothing I can do that can make any of her pain go away, but I can hope and pray that being there with her for a while helps in some small way. I do know my sisters are glad I am back in the state and will soon assume my role as the "Golden Child." As my mom always reminds us all, I am her only son. I really hope she has a speedy and complete recovery because I have promised to take her out to see her family in Philadelphia, PA this summer. I'm looking forward to road tripping with my mom, because I have a growing fear that we are running out of time to do it. She is a tough woman, but I know all of her pain is getting harder and harder to deal with. I also know that we do have a physical distance between us but the emotion and love we share has always been a part of both of us. I know I am her only son, but she is also my only mom, and I hope she is as proud of me as I am her.

302] So as I said, here I sit in Hibbing, Minnesota, living and sharing my life with some beautiful family, friends, guests, co-workers, players and students, and those of you that might be reading this book; and I can honestly say I am blessed and would have it no other way. Thanks for taking the time to listen and read some More Thoughts of a Stupid Man.

303] Before you put this book down or pass it on to someone else, please go back and read Random Thought #229. This is the point I really intended to stop writing but decided to continue, I hope I didn't go too far and I really hope you enjoyed the read. I always feel good when writing, despite what is going on in my life.

I'll steal one from Porky Pig: "That's all folks!"

THE END

EPILOGUE
OFFICIAL RESIGNATION

I hereby officially tender my resignation as an adult. I have decided I would like to accept the responsibilities of an 8 year old again. I want to go to McDonalds and think that it is a four-star restaurant. I want to sail sticks across a fresh mud puddle and make ripples with rocks. I want to think M&Ms are better than money because you can eat them. I want to lie under a big oak tree and run a lemonade stand with my friends on a hot summer's day.

I want to return to a time when life was simple, when all you knew were colors, multiplication tables, and nursery rhymes, but that didn't bother you because you didn't know what you didn't know, and you didn't care. All you knew was to be happy because you were blissfully unaware of all the things that should make you worried or upset.

I want to think the world is fair. That everyone is honest and good. I want to believe that anything is possible. I want to be oblivious to the complexities of life and to be overly excited by the little things again. I don't want my day to consist of computer crashes, mountains of paperwork, depressing news, how to survive more days in the month than there is money in the bank, doctor bills, gossip, illness, and loss of loved ones.

I want to believe in the power of smiles, hugs, a kind word, truth, justice, peace, dreams, imagination, humankind, and making angels in the snow. So, here is my checkbook, my car keys, my credit card bills, my homework, and my 401K statements. I am officially resigning from adulthood.

If you want to discuss this further, you'll have to catch me first, 'cause, "Tag, you're it!"

Gerry Levos, an ex-colleague and eternal friend, shared this with me a few years ago. I'm not sure what the source was, and I have made a few minor tweaks, but I thought it was worth sharing with anyone who has taken the time to read *More Random Thoughts of a Stupid Man*.

Mike Turnbull [Photo by Mike Flaten]

AUTHOR AUTOBIOGRAPHY

I am 55 years old and my wife Pam and I have lived in Hibbing, Minnesota for the past fifteen years. I coach and teach at Hibbing Community College, and Pam runs the Mitchell-Tappan House Bed & Breakfast in Hibbing. Pam and I own and live in the B&B, but she is the Innkeeper and I claim to be the Groundskeeper; either way, she is the boss and does a great job. Come stay with us sometime.

Pam and I have been married for thirty-two years and have two grown children. Lexie [Baack] lives and works in Nebraska with her husband Jeff. Our son Blaine lives in Minneapolis and works in a juvenile detention center at city hall in Minneapolis, MN.

I have taught and coached all over Minnesota for the past 33 years. I have cherished every minute of my career. I grew up the son of Jack and Patricia Turnbull and one of four siblings. I have three younger sisters, Terri, Lisa, and Stacie. My dad was a career Navy man, so we moved all over the country. He retired from the Navy in 1975 and we moved to Ely, Minnesota where I started my junior year of high school.

I received my A.A degree from Vermilion Community College in Ely, MN in 1979, my Bachelor's degree from Bemidji State University in Bemidji, MN in 1981, and my Master's degree from the US Sports Academy in Daphne, AL in 1990.

I had never attempted to write a book before now. I had thought about it and had been encouraged to do so by friends and family members. Now, I have written my second book and I am very excited to have the opportunity to share it with you. I hope you enjoy reading it as much as I have enjoyed writing it. It is truly a humbling and rewarding experience to put your thoughts to writing and put them out to the public.

In my 55 years on this earth, enough to qualify as an AARP member, I can't pretend to have figured anything out, but I do think I have a somewhat unique story to tell and I hope it strikes a chord with those of you who read it. I have had these random thoughts for as long as I can remember, and I've managed to write a few of them down for you to consider and ponder.

I feel blessed that Rivershore Books has agreed to publish my second book, and I look forward to future projects with them.

I have always taken pride in being referred to as "Coach," second to my favorite titles as "Husband" and "Dad." I never dreamed I would ever see "Author" in front of my name. I can only hope this might help me gain entry to the "Stupid Man" club, if and when I get to heaven.

More Random Thoughts of a Stupid Man
Mike Turnbull April 30, 2014

RIVERSHORE BOOKS

www.rivershorebooks.com
info@rivershorebooks.com
www.facebook.com/rivershore.books
www.twitter.com/rivershorebooks
blog.rivershorebooks.com
forum.rivershorebooks.com

www.ingramcontent.com/pod-product-compliance
Lightning Source LLC
Chambersburg PA
CBHW072026040426
42447CB00009B/1753